"I recommend *The Stress Factor* for every pastor and spouse, especially young pastors who often face overwhelming stresses with few resources. Yet this work is for more than pastors; it is an engaging work that will serve as an oasis-like guide for anyone walking through the arid desert of a stress-filled life."

—Dr. Phil Fuller
Superintendent, Virginia District Church of the Nazarene

"I highly recommend this book to everyone because everyone is affected on some level by stress. Further, the dangers to our mental, spiritual, and physical well-being are more than most of us realize. *The Stress Factor* works. Why? Because it is firmly grounded in biblical truth, and truth frees us."

—Brad Huddleston
International Speaker
Author of *The Dark Side of Technology: Restoring Balance in the Digital Age*
and co-author of *Forty Voices*

"Pastor Kerry and Brian have done a masterful job of demonstrating how kingdom resources might be applied to everyday stressors. I'm grateful for this resource to share with friends and clients to help them respond to stressors that come their way. We don't get to choose them, but we can decide how to respond to them and find 'real rest.'"

—Mark L. Sensabaugh
Licensed Professional Counselor

"My friends and colleagues, Dr. Brian Charette and Pastor Kerry Willis, are outstanding communicators of compelling truth. This book is filled with rock solid truth attesting to our deep need for rest and renewal in a time of turmoil and uncertainty. I highly recommend this book!"

—William F. Evans, Ph.D.
Professor of Psychology, James Madison University

THE STRESS FACTOR

The

STRESS
FACTOR

Finding Rest in an Uneasy World
BRIAN CHARETTE & KERRY WILLIS

BEACON HILL PRESS
OF KANSAS CITY

Library of Congress Cataloging-in-Publication Data
Charette, Brian.
The stress factor : finding rest in an uneasy world /
Brian Charette, Kerry Willis.
pages cm
Includes bibliographical references.
ISBN 978-0-8341-3002-9 (pbk.)
1. Stress (Psychology)—Religious aspects—Christianity. 2. Stress management—
Religious aspects—Christianity. 3. Rest—Religious aspects—Christianity.
I. Willis, Kerry W., 19691- II. Title.
BV4509.5.C443 2013
248.8'6—dc23
2012045073

10 9 8 7 6 5 4 3 2 1

To Pam, Suzanne, and Aubrey—the best stress management crew a husband and dad could ever have. Pam, you have always been a treasure to me. I'm grateful for your patience as I walked through this project. You're amazing. Family, may the Lord give me the words to communicate accurately my deep love for you always.
—*Brian*

To Kim—I am grateful to you for your love and your loyalty to our loving Lord and to me. In all the stresses of life, we know our blessings of love are much more plentiful.
To Grayson—thanks for all the front-porch talks.
To Allison—thanks for lightening life's load with your laughter.
To The Oreo Pup—thank you for being a friend,
my beloved beagle.
—*Kerry*

CONTENTS

ACKNOWLEDGMENTS

Thanks to Sharon Hardy for her willingness to tackle this project as our initial editor and Judi Perry at Beacon Hill Press of Kansas City for her patience and wise counsel throughout. The two of you made us better. As always, Mark Sensabaugh was there from the very beginning with important advice. Jennifer Testa provided much-needed encouragement at a critical time. Ultimately, it was clear to me from the start that this was a God project. This book came about because of His faithfulness. For that I'm deeply grateful.

—Brian

I wrote my first book a few years ago and honestly was pretty happy for it also to be my final book. (I signed up to preach, not to punctuate.) Yet I am delighted to be partnering with Brian Charette on this manuscript for the glory of our loving Lord and for the good of those He died to save from sin and stress. This "stress book" happened because Bonnie Perry believed it should and Brian Charette said it could. Thanks to Beacon Hill Press of Kansas City for believing in us and to the One who lives in us. I am grateful.

—Kerry

We both want to express indescribable gratitude to our local church family, First Church of the Nazarene of Harrisonburg, Virginia. We are one in the Spirit. We are one in the Lord. Unity! (John 17)

FOREWORD

Stress is a daily challenge for a lot of people. Having served as a pastor for more than forty years, I know something about the daily grind, and I remember the stress I experienced in leading a church. I was thrilled when I learned that Brian Charette and Pastor Kerry Willis were going to write a book to help those who live with stress.

I love the approach of the book and the centralized focus on Chris Seals' journey toward health, healing, and happiness. It is practical, instructive, and helpful for those who feel the pressure of living and working in the twenty-first century.

With the expertise of Pastor Kerry Willis, known as the "ultimate encourager," and the wisdom of Brian Charette, who shares counsel and the latest research, *The Stress Factor* is destined to become an oasis in the stressed-filled daily life of Christians.

I deeply appreciate the biblical approach of the authors in dealing with the matter of stress. Every Christian reader should fill his or her mind with the scriptures that have been sprinkled throughout the pages of this book and with the confidence of 1 Peter 5:7, which encourages us to cast all our cares on the Lord.

Read and relax in faith!

—Stan Toler
Author and General Superintendent, Church of the Nazarene

INTRODUCTION

You're likely thinking, *It can't be! Not another book about stress relief or stress management. Aren't there about a million of these books?* That's exactly what we were thinking when we initially prayed about whether another one was truly needed. Type "stress" in the amazon.com search field, and you get 93,356 hits. Yikes! For years, stress has been an issue that has been observed, studied, and written about.

So why another book? Isn't the horse already dead?

That's the question that drove us. Despite the millions of words that have been written on the subject—whether by scientists, counselors, pastors, or theologians—the negative effects of stress haven't gone away. The American Institute of Stress refers to it as America's number-one health problem. Maybe your family doctor has even told you that at least one of your ailments is a pure manifestation of stress.

As we write, stress is alive and quite well, contributing to personal hardships, diverted destinies, health issues, and significant levels of frustration. People need answers. Perhaps you need answers.

Since you have this book in your hands or on your screen, you or someone you love is likely dealing with issues of stress—sickness, weariness, burnout, anxiety, fear, pain.

Why is this still a problem? Why haven't we figured out how to allow God to provide healing here? What are we missing? Those are the questions we asked as we began the research and prayer that would lead to our work. We discovered three important tenets for approaching stress.

First, we have to understand the God-designed stress mechanism in us, how it works normally—a healthy response to stimuli—and how it gets short-circuited or put into harmful hyper-drive.

Second, it's important to know that a right response to chronic stress isn't passive. Simply letting stress happen to you is a dangerous decision. (And it *is* a decision.)

Third, there *is* something you can do about it, by the rich grace of God.

We believe strongly that He stands ready to meet you in this and free you from it—today.

So, yes, here we go—another book about stress.

We approach the topic in two sections. In the first section we'll tell you a kind of parable. It's the story of Chris Seal, a church leader who finds himself almost overpowered by his own particularly stress-inducing circumstances. We're sure your story isn't exactly like Chris's, but it may help you see into your own experience with stress. Chris is a man who has choices to make and fears to address. We hope that by walking alongside him for a while, you'll find points of connection and hear God's voice urging you to understand where rest, freedom, and peace can be found.

In section 2 we'll walk you through the model that Chris learns. It helps him in our story, and we believe—by God's power—it can help you. We'll introduce you to the REST tactic for taking an active approach to stress management. We'll suggest a way to think about stress and the common mistakes that increase its negative impact.

We're already praying for you.

We hope you'll find tools to use to take a step or two, maybe more, in the direction of God's destiny for you to know deeper peace and courage, walking even more closely with the only one worthy of your days.

Section 1
THE PARABLE

One

BLACK FRIDAY

● He looked up and saw the light.

Then he checked for injuries.

From his position, lying flat on his back in the First Church parking lot, Chris Seal grimaced and gingerly rubbed his ribs, testing to see if his fall on the ice did any real damage beyond embarrassment. With his other hand, he felt blindly for his keys. The way this day had gone, he wouldn't have been surprised if they had been flung into a passing truck and were now headed to Mexico.

Staring up into the glare of one of the parking lot lights, he couldn't help but wonder whether it would be best if he just stayed right there, slowly morphed by the falling snow into a white wet lump in the pavement.

Fifteen hours earlier he had been in that same position but in his warm bed watching shadows slide across the ceiling, anticipating the whine of his clock radio, listening to his wife's soft breathing, and praying that the Lord would help him prepare his Sunday School lesson early. He wanted to avoid the usual Saturday night cram session that seemed to create more stress than satisfaction.

"Cast all your anxiety on him because he cares for you" (1 Peter 5:7) read the text for the next lesson. His favorite paraphrase of that text read, "Live carefree before God; he is most careful with you" (TM). An older version read, "Casting all your care . . ."

Casting all your care.

Care. Free. Because he knew there were several in the class who really needed that message, he thought through how he might communicate that clearly—in a way they would remember. He was amazed at how harried some had allowed their lives to become. The negative effects of stress seemed to be an epidemic. He closed his eyes and prayed.

But instead of wondrous words of wisdom or quiet advice from God butterflying into his mind, the face of Daniel Wooten appeared instead.

Wooten was the new president of St. Pio's College, the small, private liberal arts school where Chris worked as Vice President of Organizational Development, a catch-all title that had him responsible for a wide array of administrative responsibilities that included a teaching assignment in the field of leadership, one of his passions.

"St. Po's," as most called it, saving a syllable, was, in many ways a small town in and of itself. Everyone knew everyone else, and each worked hard to maintain the culture that gave the school both brains and personality. Everyone loved the little community of students and educators. No one had looked forward to getting a new president.

Wooten replaced Charles Mumphrey, the man who had nurtured, cajoled, and coaxed St. Po's into becoming one of the bright lights on the small college landscape for the last twenty years. Mumphrey wasn't that much older than Chris, but he had decided to step down "while I still have the energy and passion to tend to the important things," he had said.

He certainly went out on top. The school had a solid national reputation, received three times more applicants than it could admit each year, and, shockingly, showed a healthy bottom line. Other small private schools were justifiably envious. Chris had heard Mumphrey's reasoning for walking away but wasn't sure he understood completely.

No matter. Daniel Wooten was in charge now.

"Big day today, right?" Chris turned to see his wife, Allie, leaning on an elbow and looking intently at him. She hadn't been herself for the past few days but this morning looked beautifully normal through a sleepy smile.

"I hope it's not too big," he said.

"You're meeting with Dr. Wooten? Maybe you're worried for nothing. Maybe he's going to promote you." She reached across and squeezed his arm the way she did, always searching out the best in anyone and anything.

"I guess so. But the truth is, Pip, most new college presidents want to bring in their own VP. Sometimes new presidents mean big changes. I have to be prepared to lose the best job I've ever had."

"Well, we've prayed about it. You've prayed about it, haven't you?"

He *had* prayed. Not as much as Allie, and not as much he should have, but he genuinely was trying to give this to God. Still, the tightness in his chest and sinking sensation in his stomach were raw and real. "Well, yeah, of course. But with Amy starting college and Jake three years away from starting college, I can't help worrying a little about the prospect of being on the street, résumé in hand. I mean, I'm this close to foraging for nuts and berries along the median of the Interstate."

She smiled and pushed at him. "That's pretty good for six o'clock in the morning," she laughed as they both rolled out of bed at once. "I'll have to remember that one. Hey, don't forget you're picking up Uncle Ted at the airport tonight at ten. I'm looking forward to seeing him again. I think we'll have a nice few days together."

"I'm on it. Ten."

Allie could tell that her dutiful husband's mind was drifting far from this conversation. "Babe, the fact is, God has never once let us down," she said matter-of-factly. "Never. It's what you teach all the time. I mean, have you ever regretted trusting Him in any situation?"

"No, I know," he mumbled.

"No, really," she pleaded.

He turned and looked across the bedroom at her, finding her eyes, knowing she was right and wondering what he had ever done to deserve such a gift.

•••

Daniel Wooten deserved the president's post at St. Pio. He had a strong academic pedigree featuring an Ivy League Ph.D., and he had just finished five years as president at a mid-sized public university in the Midwest. Wooten had become known for vision and innovation. He had a national reputation. It was a very positive sign when he pursued the St. Po's position with vigor. When he was a candidate for president, he spoke fondly—and, Chris believed, sincerely—in interviews about admiring St. Pio's from afar and wanting to be part of "something really special."

Chris could have put his hat in the ring for the position. Mumphrey had encouraged him, and so had the other VPs. It was obvious to all that Mumphrey had considered Chris to be next in line. Chris had grown up at St. Po's, spending most of his professional career there. While he would never acknowledge it, he was an important reason they were on the national map, recognized by several prestigious journals for their accomplishments. He just couldn't get comfortable with the concept of *President Chris Seal*. He never could get the gut-sense that it was God's will. The problem was that if he weren't willing to compete for the presidency, he had to be willing to face the prospect of losing his job entirely. Nonetheless, he refused to be a candidate if the only reason was to stay employed. Nothing about that was right.

So why was he having so much trouble with this change? Beyond the fact, of course, that it could mean his loss of employment.

Sitting in the president's waiting room mindlessly reading his diplomas and wondering what was next, he urged himself to give Wooten the benefit of the doubt. Maybe he would honor the St. Po's culture. Maybe Chris's job was safe and the two of them would form the kind of relationship he had enjoyed with Chuck Mumphrey.

Maybe not.

He would know soon enough, because Wooten had emerged from his office, buttoning his jacket.

"Hey, Chris, good morning!" he greeted from behind his perfectly knotted silk tie and bright smile. "Good to see you."

Chris was six-foot-two, and Wooten was about five-ten, Chris guessed. Still, he felt as though he was looking up at the new president. He had that kind of first-impression personality that, if not larger than life, was at least larger than you. *He even smells nice.* The fact was, he didn't know Wooten. He didn't know what was behind the smile. He just knew he wasn't Mumphrey.

I'm reacting like a six year-old, Chris scolded himself as he entered the office.

Wooten had made the space his own, rearranging the mahogany furniture and adding an odd-looking plant that appeared as if it could move on its own. A photograph on the wall showed Wooten posing with the president in the Rose Garden. (Yes, *that* president and *that* Rose Garden.) Just above that, a younger Wooten was frozen forever pulling up for a jump shot in a college basketball game. And on top of that was a drawing that one of his children had obviously made in a kindergarten art class.

The large picture window presented a view of St. Pio's central campus, now dusted white. Stone buildings formed a quadrangle with a thick lawn dotted by flowering trees that in a couple of months would give it the feeling of an orchard. Walkways crisscrossed the landscape, providing paths for the students who were now making their way to and from class. The campus was old, but not aged. It was traditional, and it was beautiful. In fact, most students who enrolled talked about the striking campus as a major influencer for them. It was stately, but it was comfortable and a place you could call home. Chris did.

At the far end of the quad, the Kennedy statue stood as a representation of one of Chris's proudest and most painful experiences.

Mary-Theresa Kennedy had struggled with an eating disorder throughout her time as a student at St. Po's. Chris worked with the Counseling Center to make sure she got all the help the staff could give her. It wasn't enough. Mary-Theresa died the summer before her senior year. When Chris heard the news, he left immediately to make the three-hour trip to the Kennedy home to be with her parents. They spent time talking about Mary-Theresa, grieving her loss and preparing for the funeral. Leafing through a scrapbook, Chris found an old picture of her holding a balloon. Five-year-old Mary-Theresa was looking up at her beautiful red floating prize with one of the brightest smiles Chris had ever seen, her hands gripping the string as if clutching hope itself. Her mother laughed through tears recounting the story of that wonderful day at the zoo. "*That* was who she was," she said.

That photo became the life-sized statue near the entrance of the quad; Mary-Theresa and her balloon. Chris was determined this was the memory he wanted St. Pio's to hold of Mary-Theresa and of all its students. There was something there that he didn't want the institution ever to forget, the buoyant spirit of a little girl, a hope out of darkness. He made it his personal passion to lead the project, raise the money, commission the sculptor, and see beauty rise from ashes.

"Beautiful, isn't it?" Wooten's voice broke in.

There was something about this meeting now that seemed hollow. The more Chris thought about it, though, the more he wondered whether that was coming from Wooten or whether, instead, it was arising from within him, an anxious ache. What was happening to him? Why was he thinking this way?

Wooten pulled a chair up beside him near the window.

•••

The new president was cordial and kind, even empathetic, but he made no guarantees about Chris's status or about the fate of any of the VPs. Bill LeVoir, the provost, had decided to step down when Mumphrey did. As a result, there would be at least one new executive officer.

But it now sounded as though there would be others. There would be change, uncertainty, and, for many, stress.

Wooten said that he had not made final decisions, but he admitted that nothing was certain and that he was still trying to get a feel for how best to build his leadership team. He wasn't making any promises one way or the other. He assured Chris that if he were replaced with a new VP, he would be given plenty of notice. He was trying to be truthful and comforting. As the meeting closed, he put his hand on Chris's shoulder, told him he knew this was difficult news, and assured him that he would always do what was best for the college.

Returning to his office, Chris replayed the meeting in his head. He appreciated Wooten's honesty and did feel respected. He had always preferred straight talk as opposed to an empty smile. Still, he had already updated his résumé-vita and had begun making contact with his network of colleagues at other colleges. Dread rolled in his gut, an ominous distant rumble. His mind raced with all that he would need to do to prepare to find a new job. Uneasiness began to fight for his attention. He fought back the creeping panic and prayed that all the activity wouldn't be necessary.

As he arrived at his office suite, he noticed that his assistant, Kim, had placed a pink phone message slip on his chair. That was her habit, since she knew that if she put it on his desk it might get lost in the jungle of papers and reports. His inbox and outbox waged daily warfare against Chris and against each other. Sometimes it got vicious.

The fact that there was only one message was unusual since Chris had become used to being greeted by a stack of messages whenever he had been away from the office for more than an hour or so.

Despite his swirling emotions, he smiled when he saw that Kent Wallace had called. Kent was Chris's pastor at First Church. He was also a dear and trusted friend. He wasn't the syrupy sweet stereotype of a blindly kind "man of the cloth" one might see in movies. He was a strong and loyal leader. He hadn't become a pastor as a fallback career. In fact, he had been a very successful management consultant before entering full-time ministry. No, Kent took to the pulpit because he was simply so passionate about Jesus Christ that it made sense to him to spend the better part of his days teaching and living the gospel. He was also very funny—milk-shooting-out-of-your-nose funny. Chris loved the opportunities he had to be around Kent.

It was because of Kent that Chris had pursued a district minister's license so that he could be more involved in the work of the church. While he considered his role at St. Po's as a ministry of sorts, Chris also liked the idea of serving in the church and training to be more effective at communicating the gospel and touching people in a meaningful way. He wanted to live his life passionately. That was one of Kent's most important influences on him.

It was no surprise that Pastor Kent Wallace had led First Church to remarkable growth and community impact during his seven years there. Chris couldn't imagine going anywhere else.

Kent and Chris's phone conversation was brief. Kent wondered if Chris would have some time to stop by the church office that evening. That wasn't unusual. The two often got together for touching-base sessions to talk about leadership, church strategy, sports, bad movies, and growing closer to Christ—not necessarily in that order. They often sought each other's advice. However, it was odd that Kent wanted to meet on a Friday evening.

Chris called Allie and gave her an update on his meeting with Wooten. She was characteristically upbeat and encouraging, later texting him with 1 Peter 5:7 and a smiley-face emoticon wearing a little skirt. He then spent the rest of the day catching up on paperwork, looking at his résumé and curriculum vitae and placing some phone calls to colleagues he hadn't spoken with recently—all while trying to ignore the ugly anxiety that seemed crouched in the corner of his office ready to pounce. He couldn't clear his mind or relax the tightening in his chest.

•••

Snow began to fall as Chris navigated late rush-hour traffic toward the First Church campus. He parked his car among the few that were remaining in the lot and looked up to see Kent's office light still on as expected. He went in through the side entrance to find his pastor waiting. He hugged Chris, perhaps a little more tightly than usual, and the two walked together upstairs to Kent's office.

"Thanks for meeting on a Friday evening," the pastor started. "I hope this didn't interrupt any plans you and Allie had tonight. Candlelight dinner? Mood music? WWE on the TV?"

Chris smiled. "Nah, Allie has a meeting tonight. Besides, I have to pick up her uncle at the airport later and didn't plan to go home anyway. And I can always DVR WWE."

Normally, this kind of back-and-forth would continue until both were satisfied they had gotten their best lines out of the way. Tonight was different.

"Okay," Kent breathed, "I've got kind of a bomb to drop on you, and I want to get right to it."

Chris had no idea where this was going, but it didn't feel good. At least it was in keeping with the way his day had gone so far. It was about to become a fiesta of bad news, and he was the piñata. "Okay," he said, hesitating. "Shoot."

"Well, you know about Angela's mom."

The two had spoken often over the last few months about what Kent and his wife, Angela, were going through. She had been burning the candle at both ends, traveling more than three hundred miles to spend time with her mother, who had been diagnosed ten months earlier with Alzheimer's disease. It had been a tough go, putting a lot of stress and strain on their family.

"I know," Chris said. "We've been praying."

"And those prayers are greatly appreciated." Kent straightened himself in his chair, glancing outside at snow dancing under the lights of the parking lot, and continued.

"We really have no idea what the future holds with Mrs. Raines. Angela is determined to be by her mother's side every step of the way."

"A six-and-a-half-hour trip one-way, four times every week," Chris thought aloud.

"Yep. And, she's a trooper of course, never complains. We've talked about moving her mom here, but familiar surroundings are very important in her care. Of course, the way things are just can't continue. So—"

At the same time that a lump caught in his throat, Chris realized what this meeting was about. He was starting to connect dots that he didn't really want to connect.

"We've decided to move to Oak Grove into Mrs. Raines' house. We'll be right there to care for her." His speech slowed, becoming more deliberate. "I'm stepping down as pastor. Other than Angela and the district superintendent, you're the only one who knows at this point. Part of me hates it. The other part knows God is in it. To cause Angela to continue to make these kinds of sacrifices would represent wildly misplaced priorities on my part."

Chris was trying to let that sink in, but the sinking was a struggle. He threw out a question just so he could continue to process.

"When?"

"Well, as soon as possible. That's kind of where you come in, buddy."

What a day this was turning out to be! Black Friday, or, since he was trying to follow Allie's model in being optimistic and hopeful, Charcoal Gray Friday.

"I would like you to pray about taking over."

Taking over? Chris felt more like falling over.

"Taking over? Taking over what?"

"The DS and I want you to pray about becoming the lead pastor of First Church—full-time ministry." If Kent had already had conversations with Dr. Daniels, the district superintendent, Chris knew this was beyond just an idea. "I've sensed for quite a while that God might be calling you. You're loved and respected by everyone in this church; you have the regard of the associate pastors, none of whom is ready for this. You're already a key leader." He had thought this through. "You're a gifted teacher with a big heart for God and His people. You certainly have the professional credentials and the appropriate licensure. Dr. Daniels asked me to supervise the transition with the district. I've prayed about it, and I think you're the guy. The fact is, we need you."

In his earlier meeting with Wooten, Chris knew what was coming. But this was beyond out of the blue. He knew all about the situation with Mrs. Raines and the pressure that it was putting on Kent. However, he always thought that Kent would find a way to balance the church, Angela's needs, and caring for their children. These were echoes of Mumphrey—another loss.

To think about First Church without Kent was rough. Add to that the thought of Chris as pastor, and all he could do was try to figure a way to slink out of the room unseen.

First Church was big and complex. It had taken the blessing of God and the expertise of Kent Wallace to build. It was making an impact in the community and actually doing what its mission statement said it would do. Leading it wasn't easy, and it was certainly not the same as leadership in a college. Chris knew that already because he had been serving in a leadership role for several years. It was fulfilling and important, but it was also challenging. It was a great place to be, but there were times when it had a herding-cats feel to it.

Yes, Chris had thought about full-time ministry, but never seriously.

"What will you do?"

"I've already had some conversations with a few former clients. We're praying for the chance to come back eventually. But we both know there's no certainty either way with Alzheimer's. Look—I know this is sudden, but I'd like to know what you're thinking."

Chris's answer was strong and confident: "Are you crazy?"

But he knew enough about God not to just laugh it off on impulse. Kent asked him to go home, talk to Allie, and carve out some time to meet with him again early the following week to address all the details. Chris knew Kent well enough to know that he had sought the Lord and had made a firm decision. He wasn't going to be talked out of leaving, but perhaps the two of them could brainstorm and determine a better choice for his replacement.

"I want you to really seek God on this. We'll be friends, no matter what decision you make. Of course, the church has no hope of success if you don't say yes, but—no pressure."

They both smiled, a little nervously.

After Chris had asked a few more detail questions, Kent wrapped his arms around him and prayed for quite some time. Then they walked together to the door.

As Chris approached his car, his mind was so occupied that he forgot to be careful of the thin film of ice underneath the now steadily falling snow. As he turned the corner, both of his feet flew forward, and he knew he had lost it—too late to do anything about a messy, slushy spill. He careened backward, but cushioned the impact of the wild fall with a flailing right hand. Still, his back slammed hard against the wet pavement, as if a hand were driving him downward.

And so he lay there, with the day's events swirling like the snow. In one day he found that he was probably losing a job he loved and was being offered one that he couldn't take. And in the middle of all that he had college tuition and a mortgage and a career in peril. Now, a biting pain was creeping from his lower back to the tips of his fingers and toes.

The snow began to settle on his chest, feeling heavier than it should have.

If he had known there was more to come, he might not have gotten to his feet.

Two

THE ARRIVAL

● Chris liked airports, but not if he had to use them.

He didn't like air travel. He knew everyone was doing his or her best, but he didn't like the crowds and delays, or cramming his long legs into spaces where long legs shouldn't be asked to go. He wasn't all that excited about the peanuts and pretzels either—although on one short-term missions trip he did entertain twenty college students by trying to make a flight-worthy paper airplane from an air sickness bag. But that was the extent of the enjoyment.

What Chris liked was visiting airports. He enjoyed knowing that he didn't have to join those fighting the crowds and surly ticket agents. He loved to watch the planes take off and land. It was somehow soothing to him.

And right now he needed soothing.

That was the reason Chris sat in his car in the short-term parking lot at the regional airport a full two hours before Allie's Uncle Ted was due just after 10:00. Snow still lightly fell, suspended under the airport's lights stretching into the night.

Normally a little airport time and deep prayer would be enough to settle his spirit and get him thinking clearly. But there was something different about how he was feeling. As he processed all he faced, he imagined various disasters. He could lose his job at St. Po's outright. He could take the First Church pastor's job out of financial desperation and create serious problems at church—*his* church. The economy had already taken a big chunk out of the college savings he had for Amy and Jake. What if things got worse? What if he had to move to find work? Could they ever sell their home in this market? If he didn't accept Kent's offer of the pastorate, who would take it, and how deeply would Kent's loss be felt? On top of those nightmare scenarios, something with Allie wasn't right, and his back was beginning to throb mightily as it stiffened. That fall in the church parking lot might have done some damage.

His heart raced. And the more he tried to calm himself, the more it pounded in his chest, as if trying to escape. On Sunday morning he would be teaching those in his Sunday School class to cast their cares on God because He cares for them. Why couldn't *he?*

This was anxiety, and he knew it. He thought of scriptures he knew well. He repeated that God had not given him a spirit of fear and even said it aloud. He reminded himself that perfect love casts out all fear and that in Christ there is a peace that goes beyond our understanding. Still, something appeared to whisper, *What if?* and his palms grew even sweatier.

He had experienced little bouts with fear in the past, but this was something new. Stronger, darker. It was as if he were in the middle of a perfect storm of circumstances, combining to push all the wrong buttons in him. He had taught that fear was the opposite of faith. Now the two were in a raging war, and he was in the middle.

"Why am I making such a big deal out of this?" He actually said it aloud, in fact a little louder than needed when alone in a car. "Lord, what is this?"

He tried Allie on her cell. She always brought him back to earth. But the call went straight to voicemail. He listened to her greeting just to hear her voice and cut off the phone.

He was alone with a thousand thoughts he couldn't control or fully understand.

• • •

Chris didn't worry about finding Ted Larson at the baggage claim. First of all, Ted was six-three. Chris would just look across the crowd and then up a few inches. Ted would no doubt have befriended someone, offered his assistance in some way, and would be helping with the luggage. On one summer visit a few years back, Ted drove around town on a Saturday afternoon determined to find every single lemonade stand being run by children in order to purchase every drop. "I'm cornering the market!" he cackled when pulling out of Chris's driveway.

He had come a long way.

"Chris!" Ted shouted Chris's name loud enough so that Chris was sure all the Chrises on the departing planes turned their heads.

Allie's uncle came up from behind and hugged Chris with his typical gusto. He was the strongest, wiriest seventy-two-year-old man that Chris had ever heard of. Chris winced as the muscles in his back contracted with the force, and his knees gave just slightly.

"Uncle Ted!" he said, turning.

"What's wrong?"

"What do you mean, 'What's wrong?'"

"I mean what's wrong?" Ted repeated, looking hard into Chris's face. "Something's bothering you."

"Doing great!" Chris said, lying.

In mock disgust, Ted turned his attention to the baggage conveyor and looked for his things. Watching the bags circle, he said to no one in particular, "You know, the old me would have said something just like that, so I get it." He smiled at Chris over his shoulder. "I've missed you. We've had some questionable types marry into this family, but you're not one of 'em."

The two made small talk until Chris recognized Ted's luggage, a deeply worn green duffle bag with gold navy pilot's wings pinned near the handle and the faded letters "POW" near the crest. Under normal circumstances, Chris would have insisted on carrying his guest's bag. But these weren't normal circumstances. Ted probably could have carried both the bag and Chris to the car if he were so inclined.

Uncle Ted's arrival was by far the best thing that had happened that day.

As the two walked side by side out of the terminal and into the cold, a plane was taking off. They turned and paused to watch it climb. Chris always wondered what memories found their way into Ted's thinking at any given moment. Anyone who had survived getting shot down twice and endured three years in a Vietnamese prison camp had some powerful memories. Chris had learned many of them over these past few years.

He was startled when Ted turned and, as if reading his mind, said, "You know which one was the worst? It was the one with the most uncertainty. That was when I was most afraid."

Neither man spoke as they found the car and navigated their way onto the main highway. Then Ted took a long breath and started.

"It was a Friday late in '64. I was a lieutenant JG flying a Guppy off the flight deck of the *U.S.S. Valley Forge*. We were the last plane to launch that day. Something happened, probably a vortex out of the plane that had just taken off. But we shifted violently to the left, dropped a wheel into the catwalk, tearing up the elevator deck, snapping off our port landing gear and mangling the flap. In what I know now was a miracle by the hand of God, we skimmed the wave tops but leveled off and actually began to climb. That was just the beginning of three-and-a-half scary hours. Scary."

For a moment he stared out the passenger window. Chris thought it was strange that as much time as the two had spent together and as much as he had learned about the man's past, this was new.

"Without landing gear, I couldn't put us back on the flight deck, so the controllers decided to send us to Oceana Naval Air in Virginia. We were so aerodynamically dirty I wondered how we could possibly make it. The aircraft shook violently the whole way. About thirty minutes in I got the dreaded 'metal chip' warning, which meant the engine was gradually coming apart. The best I could hope for was crashing into the water. That gave us a much better chance than exploding in mid-air, which was a solid bet at that point."

He paused and turned to Chris.

"I think that was the first time in my life I ever actually thought about God. I didn't really pray. Didn't know how. Just thought about whether He could actually be real. But that almost made me more afraid. It was as if being sure God didn't exist was a more comfortable stance than thinking He might."

He dabbed at his eyes with a handkerchief and continued.

"Anyway, they foamed up the runway at Soucek Field and waited for us. We knew if we could get down it would be on one good wheel. Ended up being an awful landing, but, it was a landing." He chuckled. "Just as we ran out of foamed runway, we veered off into a snow bank and came to a stop. You know, it was almost worse than being captured, because at least then I had some idea what I was dealing with. Up in the air in the shattered Guppy I had no concept of how we could possibly make it. It was the not knowing, the feeling of being stuck. That's when the pressure—and the pain—came."

Chris pulled into the driveway and turned off the engine. Both men sat quietly until Allie flipped on the front porch lights.

• • •

By the time the greetings were done, Ted had teased Amy and Jake, Allie had asked her uncle for relative updates, and everyone was finally settled, it was nearing midnight. When they were alone, she asked the question Chris had been anticipating.

"So how was your day?"

Chris actually laughed out loud. It was a laugh that sounded strange in his ears. Not funny. "It was, well, interesting."

He tried to cover it all. The less-than-hopeful meeting with Wooten, the fall, picking up Uncle Ted, and, with the most detail, his conversation with Pastor Kent. As he heard the words pour out, he was growing increasingly frustrated. Self-pity. Frustration. His face warmed. He was just about spitting by the time he had finished.

"How bad is it?" she asked, approaching him.

Full-fledged anger now. *What's wrong with me?* "How do you lose someone like Kent and keep a good church going? Just when —and how am I—"

"I wasn't talking about that. How is your back?" She felt for bumps.

"I'm fine!" he snapped, pulling away abruptly. "Everything's fine!" He was sure everyone in the house heard him. The sound of Chris's voice raised would have stopped them in their tracks.

Then a loud and awkward silence. His words echoed. He regretted them immediately. Tears welled in Allie's eyes as she approached him again.

As if there were any doubt until this moment, now they both knew things were closing in on him. He was shocked at himself for responding to her that way. He had faced stress many times, just like every other human being on the planet. But this was definitely different. He understood his fear, but now anger? This uncharacteristic eruption was a symptom of something. He knew that intellectually, but he had much less clarity emotionally. This kind of response was beneath him, yet he was living it. Fear, panic, dread. He was embarrassed, wondering how his Sunday School class would feel if they saw the great teacher in this shape.

She hugged him while he repeated, "I'm so sorry."

He had first seen her when they were both in college. Chris was a big brother to the seven-year-old son of a single mom. He took the boy to a play that Allie's church was putting on for the children in the community. She played Pippi Longstocking, and she was perfect, from the braids to the freckles to the strength. Only Allie was kinder. Allie was always kinder. After the play, she stayed in her costume, down on her knees on the stage, speaking to every child individually as if each were the only reason she was there. She had balloons for everyone, at her own expense, Chris learned later.

She stole Chris's heart before he even knew it was gone.

Now—twenty-three years of marriage, two children, countless joys, and a few sorrows later—she was still "Pip" to him.

But lately, things weren't right. The pressure had been building in Chris ever since Mumphrey had announced he would be leaving. That rocked his world more than he had expected. On top of the financial pressures he was feeling, what had started as concern was blossoming into full-blown anxiety. It was all taking its toll.

Allie wasn't herself either. Chris couldn't really explain it, but for the past few weeks it seemed as if she had been out of her regular rhythm. He had asked her several times if she were sick, or perhaps worried about Amy going off to college, or even concerned about Wooten's ultimate decision. It had to be one of those. The best way he knew to describe it was to say she was much more hesitant.

But there was no hesitancy in her voice when she said, just before he began drifting to sleep, "You'd make a great pastor."

•••

The wonderful smell and the terrible singing woke Chris and Allie on Monday morning about an hour before their alarm clock was set to go off. It was Uncle Ted, right on cue. Chris had to give him credit—the man could cook. Allie didn't love her uncle just because she knew that while he visited the meals would be prepared and the kitchen would be immaculate—but it was a nice bonus. On the other hand, the man's singing was so bad that Chris wouldn't have been surprised if some morning a moose showed up at the door with candy and flowers.

"You have to love him." Allie said sleepily, reaching over to turn on the lamp.

"Do I have to?"

"How's your back?"

"Something's wrong with me, but I think the least of it is my back." He tried to execute a graceful roll out of bed but the muscles on his left side pulled immediately, and a sharp pain leapt down his leg. Once he got to his feet, there was some relief.

In Ted Larson's world, "sleeping in" meant you were still in bed after 5:30. But in that same world, breakfast was scrambled eggs and bacon and, with any luck, the best chocolate chip pancakes Chris had ever tasted. "Breakfast like a king, lunch like a prince, and dinner like a pauper." Ted had said over and over.

He shouted from the kitchen, "Allie girl, where's the oregano?"

"It's not a secret ingredient—it's just a spice!" Chris yelled back, teasing him.

Ted had waxed poetic on many occasions about how he could tell them his "secret" scrambled eggs ingredient, but then he would have to kill them. Of course, anyone and everyone knew he put a dash of oregano and cheddar cheese in the eggs, but they let him have his pretend-mystery.

"I may be out!" Allie called back smiling and tossing her head.

Silence.

Allie grinned mischievously and waited for him to discover the small jar right where he was looking.

"Awww—here it is," he said. "Gotta admit—you almost had me. Out of oregano? Why, the thought of it!"

It had been a restless weekend. Praying and talking with Allie had helped Chris gain some perspective on the situation, and Ted was always a great listener. Nonetheless, his chest still tightened as he thought about the conversation he would have with Kent and the potential for Kim to buzz him in his office at some point with the news that "Dr. Wooten would like to see you."

There was no little irony present in the Sunday School lesson he taught. "God caring for you isn't just an idea from a greeting card," Chris lectured, referencing the 1 Peter 5:7 text. "He wants you to give those cares to Him, dropping them at His feet as if they were a bag of hammers. Being committed to Christ means you don't have to live in worry and anxiety. You can be carefree."

Yeah, irony. Or Chris was just a hypocrite, because he was worried, anxious, and now—feeling guilty too.

Several said the lesson helped them. He spent at least twenty minutes afterward praying with them. He knew that many were carrying burdens that were much greater than his. It helped him to focus on their needs rather than on his own situation.

"You meet with Pastor Wallace this evening?" Ted asked from behind Oregano Mountain.

"Yes, sir. He wants to know whether I'm at least willing to entertain the proposal and meet with the church board about it."

"What are you thinking?" Allie asked. She was working very hard to be in his corner without pushing him one way or the other.

"You know what's got me by the throat right now?" he asked them. "What I don't want is to be forced out at St. Po's and consider taking Kent's place just because I need a source of income. I also don't want to enter into full-time ministry for what seems like a thousand wrong reasons from wanting to support Kent to being worried about the church. It has to be something I can clearly sense God doing. It's also driving me crazy that it's all driving me crazy. I mean, what's wrong with me?"

"Allie," Ted said, "make a note not to ask him what he's thinking anymore." Then without missing a beat, he led them in a prayer.

•••

It helped that his Monday was full. He had several meetings and taught his leadership development class prior to his meeting with Kent at their favorite place, an old diner downtown that had actually been a railroad car. Calling it a dive would be an insult to dives everywhere. But the coffee was good, and the place was quiet. Kent often added that the rodents seemed relatively clean and well-mannered.

"Tell me again, why me?"

"Well, I've asked about ten other people, and you're all I have left," Kent teased. "Look—I realize this has you reeling a little."

"Just a little."

"But it really shouldn't be a surprise. People look up to you. I get the e-mails from your class, and just about everyone from St. Pio's comes to First Church. You're a gifted, selfless man. You understand leadership and always put everyone else ahead of yourself. You're a terrific teacher and, frankly, I've been to the Lord on it, and I believe you're His choice. And you know I don't kid around when it comes to this church."

"What about Ed?"

"Ed's a terrific associate pastor, and the kids love him. But he's twenty-five years old and just isn't ready. He would tell you himself."

"Greg?"

"I thought of Greg. But we both know his days as senior pastor are over. He loves his niche with the shepherding team, but he really wants to be a follower at this stage of his career. And he's a great follower. Let me ask you what's so hard to grasp about my choosing you?"

"Well, for one thing, I'm not a pastor."

"Not yet anyway."

"You know what I mean."

"And you know what *I* mean. Before I was the pastor of First Church, I wasn't a pastor. I was a seventy-hour-a-week management consultant near the end of my rope. One of my closest pastor friends was in banking before he accepted his call, and another was in advertising. Advertising! In my case it was 'Here I am, Lord—send me.' And that's exactly what He did. I haven't regretted a single day. Best years of my life."

"And we're all better for it."

"Now what about you?"

"That's what I've been asking."

A couple with three young children bounced into the diner, the rust-grease bell on the door unceremoniously announcing their arrival. Chris recognized them from First Church.

"Pastor Kent!" the children called out in unison, climbing into the booth and all over the pastor. He gathered them to him and called each by name.

"What brings you to this place?" Chris asked, saying "this place" as if referring to a dumpster.

"We love the grilled cheese here!" said the wife. "It's our little secret. The first Monday of the month is grilled cheese Monday."

Seeing the family light up in Kent's presence was a painful reminder to Chris of just whom he would be replacing, if he could. But that in itself was a problem. There was something wrong in his thinking. Rather than seeing Kent with these precious children as a moment in time full of joy, he turned it into a negative, a self-critical comparison between Kent and himself. What was that all about?

The young family headed for their corner table and grilled cheese heaven while Chris and Kent reassembled their booth.

"What I'm really struggling with is how I'm handling this," Chris explained, "or not handling it. I have always been able to keep things in perspective, to trust the Lord with whatever's next, and not to get too overwhelmed by life. I'm always the one in control."

"That's true."

"But, for some reason, not this time. I mean I just about chewed Allie's head off last night talking about it. Something's wrong with me."

"You're under a great deal of stress. I know this decision I've put in front of you hasn't helped that."

"But I've been under stress before, many times."

"But this isn't like other times. You can't just assume that the way you've always handled things can be automatically applied to every situation. This is a unique moment that calls for a fresh trust in God. New thinking. No one can blame you for feeling the pressure. Truth is, I would be worried if you weren't just a little nervous."

"Well, I'll say this—God's got my attention."

"Then you're in a good place."

The two men talked details until the grilled cheese group was almost finished with their lime Jell-O. Chris had asked and Kent had answered just about every conceivable question.

"I don't need a final decision today, of course. But I do need to know if you're willing to meet with the board to at least begin to explore the possibilities. It will be very important that the board hear your heart and give an endorsement to the district superintendent.

Angela and I are going to put our house on the market soon; the moment of truth is approaching."

Chris didn't feel pushed or pulled. He felt more drawn, strangely intrigued, and, for a moment, at peace. "I'm willing to meet with the board. At least I'm not ready to say no."

Driving home from the diner, Chris punched up the voicemail messages on his phone. All three were from colleagues at St. Po's, and all three asked him the same question. Had he heard that Wooten was having dinner that night with two of his former VPs? *Had they made the long trip just to have dinner, or were they talking about jobs at St. Po's? Were they talking about his?*

Three

STRESSORS

● At the end of the day on Thursday, with everything else that was going on, Chris found himself sitting on the thin paper covering of the examination table in his doctor's office looking at a jolly cartoon spine on the wall. "Spiney"—Chris didn't know if that was his real name or a nickname—had obviously been designed to teach children about back injuries. The healthy Spiney was smiling brightly. The injured Spiney was wincing and holding his back, which was a little bit odd if you thought about it, a spine having a spine. That's what occupied his mind as he waited for his friend and doctor, Sam Morgan, to return.

Chris looked forward to going to the doctor in the same way he looked forward to traffic court. But he had known Sam for years and trusted him. Since falling in the church parking lot, Chris was getting worse instead of better. He was waking up every day with unusual stiffness and pain and had even developed a noticeable limp. If it were up to Chris, he would just wait it out, justifying it as the slowed recovery time due to aging. When he was twenty playing Division II college basketball, he would jam a sprained ankle into a bucket of ice for an hour and be back on the court the next night.

Alas, he wasn't twenty. And further, it wasn't up to him. Allie had insisted that he get looked at. Sam had poked, prodded, frowned, and left the tiny room to consult with one of his colleagues.

As he leafed through a *Redbook* magazine from the early eighties, Chris heard a text message pop up on his phone, which was in the pocket of his pants that were draped across one of the chairs in front of Spiney. It was from Kent. "Confirming board meeting set for 6:30 tomorrow. You'll be great!" It wasn't news, since Kent and Chris had spent an hour the day before mostly talking about Chris's idea about a new clothing distribution center in the church and praying together about the board meeting. Seeing it in writing made it more official, perhaps more ominous.

A knock on the door got his attention. It was Sam. Chris thought it was refreshing that Sam always knocked on the examining room door before just walking in. Technically, Chris supposed, he could have just barged on in. It was his examining room, after all.

"Okay, buddy," Sam started. "Got two concerns I want us to do something about."

"What's up?"

"Well, first, your blood pressure is high, and not just a little high—146 over 84."

"Wow. That *is* high. That usually isn't a problem for me."

"Yep. That's why we need to pay attention to it. Have you been under some stress lately?"

"That would be an understatement. But I'm usually much better at handling it. Just seems as though I'm more burdened with life than normal."

"What are you doing about it?"

"Well, I haven't thought about actually doing anything about it, although Allie's uncle seems to have some ideas. I pray and I try not to stress out. Easier said than done, though."

"I understand completely. Actually, stress isn't something you can just accept passively. A lot's been written about it in the medical literature over the past few years. It can be pretty dangerous if you don't take an active response. It's not a good idea to just let it *happen*."

"I hear you."

"Anyway, I want you to pick up one of these at-home blood pressure sensors, and I want to see you again if you can't get it into the 120s and 70s consistently. I also want you to read through this material on stress."

"Got it. You said there were concerns, like—more than one."

"Right. The second is that pain you're experiencing in your lower back. I don't like how things feel back there."

"Believe me—neither do I."

"Yeah, that's funny. Haven't heard that one before," Sam said, grinning. "So I'm ordering an MRI. I want to get a closer look at it. It may be more than just a strain."

Sam handed him several more documents—the MRI order, a prescription for the pain, and a pamphlet on Bible verses that address healing.

"By the way, Sam, how's Lydia doing?"

Lydia was Sam and Becky's twelve-year-old daughter. She had been born with Down's Syndrome and lit up every room she entered, the girl with the thousand-watt smile. But she was facing some very serious heart surgery, and Chris knew it had been weighing on Sam.

"She's doing great, usually handles things better than her mother and me. Surgery's scheduled for next week."

"Let's pray for her right now."

Chris reached over and put a hand on Sam's shoulder, and the two men prayed for Lydia Morgan. Chris tried to ignore the sound of the beating of his own heart getting strangely louder.

•••

"He's absolutely right, you know," Ted concluded. "Stress isn't something you can be passive about."

Chris smiled as he took the sage advice from a man dressed in jeans, navy pilot boots, a "Real-Men-Love-Jesus" t-shirt, and a "Mug-the-Cook" apron, standing over a pot of chili.

"Who said that?" Jake asked as he carried bowls to the dinner table.

"Your dad's doctor," said Allie, following him with a salad.

"Dad went to the doctor?" Amy joined in.

"Yep. High blood pressure," Ted said.

"I'm so glad my medical report is the subject of dinner table conversation. Anyone else want to add anything?"

"I'd be happy to talk about my gallstones," Ted offered. "Or that time I ruptured my spleen."

"Let's just pray so we can eat and talk about things that are a little more pleasant." Allie was always the voice of reason.

Chris asked the blessing, but the dialogue didn't stop. He tried to divert the discussion by pointing out that Allie wasn't eating again, but to no avail.

"Is there anything we should be concerned about?" Amy asked.

"No, Honey, just a lot going on. I meet with the church board tomorrow, and Dr. Morgan is a little concerned about my blood pressure and about this back injury. I'll be fine."

"A very wise man once told me to trust God with your whole heart and to treat your own knowledge with a healthy skepticism," Jake said.

"Sounds like you've been talking to Solomon," said Ted wryly.

"It's my dad's paraphrase. The R-S-V, 'Revised Seal Version.'"

"Well, they're both right." Ted turned to Chris. "I don't suppose you've ever heard of the REST stress response tactic?"

"REST?" Chris said.

"Yep. R-E-S-T. REST. It was a God-send to me."

Chris knew that if anyone had experienced his share of stress, it was Ted Larson. This man had been through more than anyone Chris had ever known. Two tours in Vietnam, countless flights behind enemy lines, POW, high level hush-hush job in naval intelligence, losing two wives to cancer. And that was just a start. When Ted talked about being "saved" by Christ, he meant it literally. And yet with all that, he was probably one of the most truly content, truly joyful men Chris knew. The love of God was all over him, and everyone knew it, no matter what he faced.

"It was probably twenty-five years ago now," Ted recalled. "It was just after Mary's passing, and it was as if the world was bearing down. I remember there were times when it felt like I actually had to stop and remember to breathe. I gotta admit—I wasn't sure I wanted to live anymore."

Chris glanced at Amy and Jake's facial expressions. Neither had known the before-Christ Uncle Ted, before his life changed. It must have been strange for them whenever he spoke about that time.

"I got roped into going to a pilot's reunion, probably two hundred fifty of us or so. But for a reason I didn't understand then, I got put at the table with all the doctors. I'm sitting there surrounded by these guys talking about flying and surgery, like they were one and the same. The conversation turned to stress, because this one guy had spent his whole career studying it. He talked about the nature of stress, differences between types of stress, PTSD—"

"Post-traumatic stress disorder," Jake said.

"Yes, sir. So as these guys are all talking, I'm sitting there realizing that they're talking about me. I could tick off all of the symptoms of stress they listed—anxiety, depression, worry, sudden anger, mood swings, irritability, headaches, muscle problems. I was even worrying about worrying. It really struck me when one of them said that he believed that most physical disease could be tied to stress in some way. Most! And this was twenty-five years ago. They know a lot more now."

"So what about R-E-S-T?" Chris asked.

"That came later. After the dinner, I made an appointment with Mark Huddleston, one of the doctors. I just seemed to click with him and wanted to talk about what I was going through. No-nonsense guy. Liked him from the start. I didn't notice 'till later that he had both the medical insignia *and* the chaplain's cross on his uniform. The first appointment turned into many meetings, and those many meetings turned into friendship. The long and short of the story is that Mark Huddleston is the man who told me about Christ and about REST. I'll be forever grateful to him."

"Uncle Ted, I'd love to hear more, but I have a meeting with my AP History study group—I gotta go," said Amy.

"Well, I'm on the verge of boring everyone anyway. We'll pick it up again, and I can tell you about REST."

Thirty minutes later, they had each left the table except Chris. And it wasn't just because his back made sitting his most comfortable position. He had retrieved his yellow legal pad from his briefcase and had started to make notes about what had been occurring in his life and how he had responded to it. As much technology as Chris used, he was most comfortable tracking his studies on a legal pad. He even sketched a timeline, marking each stress-producing event. At the bottom of the page he wrote in large capital letters *"REST?"* Under that he wrote "Proverbs 3:5, Matthew 11:28-29, Philippians 4:7, 1 Peter 5:7."

•••

That Friday morning began with one of Chris's favorite meetings. He had started a mentoring program at St. Pio's that put faculty members together with small groups of students who had a common challenge. One group consisted of young women from lower socioeconomic status, another of male students who were fatherless, and so on. There were seven such groups. Chris's group consisted of five young men who suffered some kind of disability, from Marc, who had learning challenges, to Seth, who had mild cerebral palsy, to Shane, who was dyslexic. Although Chris had developed the program and was considered the leader of the group, he knew that he had benefited from the relationships at least as much as the young men had. He told Allie that his only responsibilities in that group were to love and serve each one, more as a friend than as a professor or administrator. He loved it.

This particular day the group was a bay of peace in a season of storms.

As the young men were leaving the office, Dr. Wooten was in the hall talking with Kim. He smiled in Chris's direction and nodded his head, indicating that he would like to see him. Chris said his last goodbyes to the students and ushered Wooten into the office to sit at the small conference table.

"Chris," Wooten said smiling, "I don't want to take a lot of your time, but I want you to know that I know who you are." Chris tilted his head like a dog encountering algebra. "And I know what I'm putting you through."

"It's really—"

"No, I need to say this. Should have said it before. I realize what kind of man you are and all you have meant to this institution. You've really touched a lot of lives here. You don't like to talk much about your accomplishments, I've learned that, but there are plenty who do. And believe me—they've let me know how important you are around here. Some have said, in not so many words, that you should be the one in my office."

Chris was squirming internally. He wasn't great with such praise and wasn't sure where it was leading. As Wooten continued, he heard a text come to his phone with Allie's ring. He wondered what was up but wasn't about to interrupt Wooten in the middle of whatever it was that was happening.

Wooten fumbled with his pocket square, perhaps the first gesture Chris had seen that was less than completely poised and professional.

"I also realize what an unfair position you're in. A man of your caliber should be assured of his place at St. Pio's for well into the future, not worrying about whether the new president will replace you. But you've handled it all flawlessly."

If only he knew.

"So the simplest thing for me to do would be to tell you you've got the job for as long as you want it. But I also know from experience it's not as simple as that for several reasons. We're going to change, as you know. We have to adapt to the future higher education marketplace."

"Absolutely."

"And although we're strong financially, we don't have unlimited budget. So I can't just add to my leadership team without some consideration of the cost."

He was right, of course.

"I don't think it's wise for me to be making any major decisions just now. I should be asking a lot of questions, learning as much as I can, understanding the critical issues. Listening."

"Dr. Wooten, I don't disagree with anything you've said, and I really do understand."

"But I also know that none of this changes the fact that you and the other VPs are in a very difficult position, and I know it must be weighing on you. I care about that too."

Chris's shoulders relaxed a little.

"So I promise I will let you know something by the end of the month. This will not drag on forever. In fact, I'd like to set a meeting with you in three weeks. I'm committed to being able to provide you with a proposed decision and an explanation of my thought process. I hope you understand that the most important thing on my mind is to make decisions that lead to the brightest future possible for St. Pio's. Everything else is secondary."

Chris couldn't argue with any of it. As he sat and listened, he prayed for Daniel Wooten.

"Now before wild rumors get out there, I want you to know that I did have two former colleagues in this week, and I walked them around the campus. It was *not* a job interview, but in the interest of transparency, there is some potential there. They are both high-character, high-talent men who have a long track record of success."

And one of them could be my replacement.

"But at this stage there are no job openings, and I was careful to let them know that. I don't want you to think I'm sneaking around. It's simply a matter of integrity for me. I want to earn your trust."

Chris knew that this was the best Wooten could do. And he appreciated it. If Chris had been in his place, it would be all that he could do as well. Any new CEO is wise to do more listening than talking, more observing than decision-making. It was the better part of wisdom. The downside, of course, was that no one was really certain about the future, no one absolute about his or her long-term employment status. But as a follower of Jesus Christ, Chris knew that none of that should be his primary thought anyway. He knew it. He had told his wife, his children, his friends, his Sunday School class, to trust God and not get all wrapped up in their own circumstances.

He reached for his phone to get Allie's text. She sent "Proverbs 3:5" followed by a smiley face. He knew it, of course. "Trust in the LORD with all your heart and lean not on your own understanding."

He repeated it to the queasy feeling in his gut. *Trust?*

• • •

Chris's car was a running joke at St. Pio's. It wasn't new or shiny, and it didn't have all of the bells and whistles. In fact, Chris was sure it didn't have any whistles. But it got him from point A to point B, as he always noted proudly. The fact that Chris never had the best vehicle was a product of a decision he and Allie had made soon after getting married. They wanted to tithe to the church, of course, but they also wanted to be able to do more, figuring that ten percent just didn't sound like much when you were talking about honoring the very Lord of the universe. As a result, they determined that they would never borrow money for a car and that they would consider the difference between whatever they drove and what would be considered "normal," and give that to the church each year. It had worked wonderfully, but it resulted in each of them driving vehicles that elicited smiles from those who watched them pass. Chris always made sure that Allie had the nicest of their cars, but even that wouldn't impress anyone.

So when Chris headed out for lunch with Ted, it didn't shock him that his car had trouble starting. What did shock him was how he responded. Usually, he just smiled, prayed, and asked the car politely to start. It hardly ever failed. But today as he cranked the ancient engine, he found himself getting angry. In his head, he was cursing the stupid decision to drive this heap. There were strange rumblings in his heart. He slammed his foot down on the accelerator and raised his hand to pound the steering wheel into submission, but stopped and thought, *Where is this coming from?*

Eventually, both he and the car rebounded and headed to the airport, where Ted had asked to meet him. As he maneuvered through noontime traffic, encountering good drivers and those who apparently were blindfolded, he found himself more frustrated than normal. More stressed.

As it turned out, eating a beef-and-bean burrito on the wing of a plane was just the kind of lunch break Chris needed that day. He and Ted sat with their legs dangling from the leading edge of the wing of a 1979 Cessna 340A eating convenience store Mexican food. Ted had an agreement with the plane's owner that he could go flying in exchange for some maintenance and fuel. Ted had friends everywhere he went.

And, of course, Chris loved the airport. A hangar lunch was right up his alley.

"I want to know more about the REST stress tactic," Chris said as Ted put his tools away.

"Sure. Have you heard from your doctor on your MRI results yet?"

"Not yet. I know you can't wait to put them up on your Facebook page. Now let's go—what's this REST model? I can't find it in any of the medical literature."

"I'm guessing that's because Mark isn't the publishing type. But I've never forgotten it."

"Prove it."

Ted smiled and folded an oily rag.

"Well, like I said, one of the most important things I've learned is that you can't just let stress happen to you without some response. A bad stress response is like losing your engine at fifteen thousand feet. Doing nothing is not an option."

"You know what you just said, right?"

"I know exactly what I just said. Right now you're in a tough time with a lot of stuff going on. Future is uncertain, fear and anxiety are everywhere—the job, the church, college tuition, your back, the MRI, the step you've lost on the basketball court."

"Not so sure about the last one, but go on."

"So you were created to respond to that stuff. That's part of what makes you human. In fact, your mind and body are God-designed to respond to stress. It keeps you safe. But sometimes that response gets broken. Lots of times we break it. I know that's happened to me. I think I can honestly say that except for God's grace, it's almost killed me a time or two. Mark was the first person I heard call it 'chronic stress.'"

"I gotta say, it's a little embarrassing that you've endured all you have over the years and I'm all wrapped around the axle because of what seem like little things."

"Oh, son, they're not little at all. What you're going through matters. I think God designs our trials because they're the best trials for *us*, but that doesn't mean mine are harder than yours. That's all up to God deciding which anvil will shape us best. But any anvil is hard."

"That sounds familiar."

"Yeah, you taught me that as a matter of fact."

"REST?"

"Okay, REST is R-E-S-T, four tactics for approaching stress in a way that's aligned with God's design for your life. You know—healthy. Like I said, for me it's been a godsend. Mark told me he developed it with a study of Matthew 11:28 and 29, along with his friend's years of medical research on stress. He continues to polish it, especially with the new stuff they're learning about how we respond to stress."

"'Come to me, all you who are weary and burdened, and I will give you rest. Take my yoke upon you and learn from me, for I am gentle and humble in heart, and you will find rest for your souls'" Chris said.

"Spoken like someone who is weary and burdened. And it makes complete sense because when I have felt real bad stress—I'm talking about fear, anxiety, worry, even depression—it's always as though it's coming from a place deep inside. Like my soul itself was burdened."

"So does the R in REST stand for—*rest*?"

"Not quite. The R is the first step. *Recognize* stressors when you see them, and their potential to hurt you, and *realize* that experiencing stressors is normal. It's part of life."

"Recognize and realize."

"What Mark found was that Christians especially sometimes acted surprised when they faced trials or challenges or hardships, as if they were somehow surprised by suffering. They were under the wrong impression that the Christian life was supposed to be stress-free, trouble-free. As if it's all smooth flying—no turbulence."

"Suffer with Him; reign with Him."

"Right."

"So what's the big deal about recognizing stress or realizing it's normal?"

"Good question. First of all, what you're recognizing are the *stressors*—those things that can cause negative stress if you don't respond right. The way you think about stress matters."

"So you make a distinction between a stressor and stress?"

"Definitely. The stressors are all around you. They're normal. Tough diagnoses, hard decisions, broken relationships, sad circumstances, overdrawn bank accounts. Some call them trials and tribulations. Everyone faces them, including Christians."

"Especially Christians."

"And especially leaders, like you."

Ted peeled a banana as if performing surgery. Then he bit off a big chunk and grinned. The creases around the old pilot's mouth and eyes were talking to him.

"Funny thing is, some things that are fun for some are stressors for others," Ted continued, swallowing. "I love to fly—great relaxation."

"And I'd rather have a nice root canal."

"Exactly. And you're always getting up in front of people and teaching."

"Which you probably don't prefer."

"Yeah, that's right, if by 'don't prefer' you mean *hate*. Scares me to death. What stresses you is what stresses *you*."

That made sense. What Chris didn't know was whether his stress was the result of the sheer number of challenges he was facing at the moment or the unique combination of threats he sensed. His guess was that it really didn't matter if his response was not aligned with God's purposes. No matter the reason for the stress—he knew he had to start making better choices about his response.

"So you have the stressor," Ted continued, swallowing, "whatever is causing a response in you. And then you have *stress*, which is the word we usually use to talk about our un-God responses to those stressors."

Chris rolled the term "un-God" over in his brain. "So recognize stressors as they're happening to you."

"And how you're responding to them."

"Right. And realize that the fact that those things being in your life is normal—nothing wrong with you."

"Right. And you can't take an active stance against a bad stress response until you can identify where the stress is coming from. You have to be able to say, 'I'm feeling this way because this is happening,' and make a connection. You want to be on the offensive when it comes to stress. Attack. You can't just let a bad stress response happen and resign yourself to fear, depression, that stuff."

Through the huge hangar doors, Chris watched another plane land. The information wasn't necessarily new, but it was making sense in a way that it hadn't before. And it definitely applied to him. "Okay—you have to be aware that it's happening and the potential dangers. But why is realizing it's normal so important?"

"Well, first, because that's where the right response starts. But also because the way you think about your stressors can make things worse."

"How so?"

"Well, I've heard you say you're frustrated because of the way you've responded to some of these things."

"I am. I should know better."

"So you feel out of control."

"Oh, definitely."

"Well, see? That's it. You're *stressing about stress!* You're feeling anxious about how you've been responding. Your stress causes you to snap at Allie, so you're angry at yourself, even more stressed, because of that response. So the question of whether you should take the pastorate is creating a negative stress response in you—fear, anxiety, worry, high blood pressure. The sick feeling in your gut. Your stress response just keeps firing because you're *making* it fire. Then you add to that the fact that you don't understand why you haven't responded better, like your world is spinning, and that multiplies the stress."

"Or when I get angry for seemingly no reason and get confused about the anger."

"Sure."

"So the idea is to be able to say, 'This decision is a stressor, and I'm not responding to it in a good way.'"

"Even better if you say that to God and ask Him to help you as a first step. You start with Him. God's voice, God's will, God's comfort. He's at the heart of *all* peace and security. Keep a running dialogue with Him about the burdens in your life. Tell Him He can have them!"

● ● ●

Chris had been to many church board meetings over the years. In fact, before he received his district license, he had served on the board. He knew each person and appreciated each one's commitment to Christ and to the local church. Still, that afternoon dragged by and his sense of dread grew, anticipating that night's meeting, a special session called to discuss Kent's resignation and Chris's decision.

Kent had spoken individually with each board member about the decision. Since everyone loved the pastor, the responses were similar. They were deeply disappointed to be losing him but understood his decision. Of course, the suggestions were numerous: moving Angela's mother, setting up a commuting arrangement, continuing to preach on Sunday but being away Monday through Friday were all discussed. In the end, though, each board member admired Kent's commitment to Angela and knew that he was practicing the behavior he had always preached—an unwavering passion for Christ and an unflinching loyalty to family, in that order.

Chris's Sunday School classroom was set up in a large U-shape with Kent, Angela, Chris, and Allie sitting together in the open end of the U facing the board members. Dr. Daniels, the district superintendent, sat to the left of Kent. Chris had had several opportunities to interact with the DS. All Chris needed to know about Dr. Daniels was that at the age of sixty he had volunteered to lead the youth group at his church and was great at it. He was kind and wise. Some leaders at his level of authority might have added tension to a meeting like this. Not Dr. D.

Allie was busy talking to her friends, who were many, as people settled into their seats. When you engaged Allie, you always got a hug, a smile, and a listening ear. Chris was sure there were some who were just as excited about her potential new role as they were about Chris's.

This meeting has the potential to cause a negative response in me. Lord, guard my heart against fear and anxiety. I'm facing a stressor here. I want what you want more than I want anything. Allie eventually sat down and squeezed his hand. Could she tell he was working on "R"?

Chris and Allie had eaten dinner at their favorite restaurant at Ted's insistence. Times alone with her always had an encouraging impact on Chris—just the sound of her voice. They talked about his back, and she joked that she was having some aches as well. She called it "sympathetic back pain." Chris reported on his lunch with Ted and the REST tactic, or at least the first step. As always they talked about Amy and Jake. But mostly they talked about the board meeting and the decision. Chris was glad Allie would be there, not just for the comfort it would provide for him but also so she would see it as their decision and not just his. In the end they agreed that, like Moses, the two of them didn't want to go anywhere God wasn't.

After praying for what turned out to be an extended period, Kent started the discussion. "Thanks for being here, especially for a special Friday night session. I know what we have to talk about is important. You already know my situation, and I have appreciated your prayers. Tonight is about the future and God's destiny for First Church. You know Dr. Daniels; he's asked me to guide the meeting tonight."

Chris was having trouble reading everyone. Some of his closest friends seemed comfortable and in a kind of I'll-support-you-no-matter-what posture. He wasn't so sure about some others. Strange—he didn't even know if he wanted the job, but he caught himself hoping that they wanted him.

Make up your mind.

"Chris and Allie have been part of our church family for years, not just as members but also as leaders. I've sensed for some time that Chris might have a call to full-time ministry. He loves God and he loves people, and he is one of the most gifted men I know. But he's also a key leader at St. Pio's, and they depend on him too. We've been happy to share him. But now I think it's time for St. Pio's loss to be our gain. As most of you know, with Dr. Daniels' blessing, I've asked Chris to pray about taking over for me as lead pastor. This isn't a spur-of-the-moment decision. Angela and I have been considering this for some time." He paused, looked at each board member, and then turning, said, "Chris?"

Chris was expecting a little more ramp-up time before he had to say anything. He looked at Allie. "Allie?"

She laughed, as did the board members. That helped.

After discussing what an honor it was to be considered for the job, Chris talked about the situation at St. Pio's and his fear of looking at the First Church pastorate as a "safety net" and how he wanted to avoid that at all costs. He made reference to his medical issues, although he didn't reveal all his concerns. Finally, he told them how much he and Allie loved the church and their concerns about trying to fill shoes that really couldn't be filled. "We all know Kent's a great man. It's intimidating to think about following him in leadership."

As he spoke, his eye caught movement at the door to the classroom, as if someone were out in the hall. Since all the board members were sitting right in front of him, he knew that it wasn't a late arrival. Still, he saw someone.

"Chris, I don't want you to take any offense here, but, Kent, isn't the idea to groom the associates to be ready to take over for you?" Scott Hampton asked the question many must have been thinking. The nodding heads gave that away. Scott was a relatively new board member, a St. Po's alumnus who worked with the FBI. Maybe this wasn't going to be as smooth as Chris hoped.

"Ultimately, that's the goal, Scott," Kent said. "But there was no way to anticipate what would happen with Angela's mother—and no way to prepare for it. At this moment in time, the associates aren't ready."

"But, why—"

"But I see Chris as God's choice, and I think I would feel the same way even if we were five years down the road. God has prepared him, and if he'll take the job, I believe he's the right man. He's God's man for such a time as this. And the fact that he'll be surrounded by a ready staff of great associates is just a plus."

The last thing Chris wanted was for the meeting to break into a pro-Chris faction versus a pro-anyone-else faction. And while it wasn't quite there, it was still less comfortable than he was wanting. Kent was still speaking to Scott and side conversations had surfaced. Someone said, "Chris is a great leader, but I think we'd all feel better if we knew he wanted the job."

Well, here's a stressor if I've ever seen one.

"Chris, is God calling you to be our pastor?"

The question that rose above the chatter was from Peggy Sharpes, one of the longest-tenured board members. To describe Peggy as "no-nonsense" bordered on flowery. She was tough and smart but didn't have much patience for those who didn't take their faith completely seriously. Chris knew Peggy, because she always found her way into Chris's Sunday School class. She didn't always engage, but she was always there. Peggy had taken over her husband's small tech company when he was killed by a drunk driver five years earlier and had built it into one of the most successful firms specializing in writing applications for smart phones and tablets. At forty, she was considered one of the most influential tech-industry CEO's, and her company had a bright future. She had guts, if not grace; power, if not patience.

"Well, Peggy, I guess that's the issue," Chris said.

"Well, yes, Chris, I guess it is." She sounded impatient but almost always did. "Have you heard from God on this? We all love Pastor Kent. I know he has meant a lot to me. But I don't think he's going to change his mind, which means our most important concern is who takes his place. And our work for the gospel is much too important for hesitancy or even false modesty."

Allie squeezed his hand until, frankly, it hurt.

"Peggy, I don't think—" Kent said, obviously about to attempt a rescue operation.

"No, Peggy's right." Chris could handle this; He was in R-mode. Peggy was looking at Chris, some board members looked at Kent, and the rest now were checking to see if the carpet needed to be replaced. "As a church we're in a difficult situation, and we have to recognize the challenges this presents and understand the right response and the wrong response. The path of least resistance is most likely the wrong response, to act out of fear or selfishness. The right response will take some work, and I'm willing to do that work, whether I'm the new pastor or not."

"Say more."

"Well, as you well know, in our secular jobs we usually treat challenges by reaffirming our mission and vision and creating a strategic plan that's informed by reliable data. We try to be proactive rather than reactive. We use what we know to align our objectives with our enduring purpose. At First Church we can and should do all of that, but we should start by asking God the questions before we look to each other for the answers. Then we make decisions that are inspired by the Holy Spirit and not because we're afraid of what might or might not happen. This can't be forced, no matter how urgent things seem. You agree, Peggy?"

"Well, yes. I guess I do."

"Lead on," said Kent, smiling.

"I suggest that, together, we take some time to fast, pray, and think about what God is saying. Obviously, that's going to be personal for me because I'm the one who's been asked to take Kent's job. But it's personal for all of us because we care about the future of our church. We know we have important work to do, for an audience of one."

"We'll get together again in, say, a week?" Kent asked.

Heads nodded, smiles returned, and the figure in the hall was no longer there. There was continued discussion of options, how it all should be communicated, and what the next meeting would look like.

"All right—everyone in this room needs to spend time on his or her knees," Peggy said, somewhat softened. "So tell us how we can pray for you specifically, Chris."

"Two things, I think—clarity and REST."

●●●

Chris's anxiety and Peggy Sharpes's arrows notwithstanding, it was hard to view the meeting as anything other than a positive. At least they seemed to be moving in the right direction, even if Chris couldn't say that he was feeling much better about things. After he made the suggestion to pray and fast for a week, there had been more meaningful dialogue. Did he feel as if the board were giving him a ringing endorsement? No, but the leader in him thought that was the best approach. If he had been on the board, he would have wanted to have found a clear, unified pathway, not the first one that came around. As strange as it sounds, it helped him that they didn't lift him up on their shoulders and carry him around the parking lot shouting his name. But it also helped that they weren't repulsed by the idea of *Pastor Seal* either.

Chris opened the car door for Allie, who winced her way into the front seat. She really was having some back pain of her own. *We're like two eighty-year-olds.* He made his way around to the driver's side and started the car.

"Well, what did you think?" he asked her.

"I thought you were great!"

"You'd say that if I fell out of my chair mumbling and spitting up."

"First, gross. Second, you are my flawless dream hunk-a-rama."

"Be honest."

"I am! If I thought it hadn't gone well, I would tell you." She looked at the notes she had made. "I thought you kept things focused on the Lord and His will rather than getting into personal opinions. You came off as very confident, particularly with your handling of Peggy. If anything, I think the way you handled it actually may have enforced the idea that God is calling you."

Chris winced.

"I also think it would have been too rushed to have made any kind of decision tonight. The board members need to own this transition."

"And you?"

"I think you're a great man and will support you no matter what you are—respected higher education leader, lead pastor, paper-hatted fast-food clerk."

"The paper hat is a good look for me."

"Uncle Ted would be proud."

"Speaking of Ted, did you—"

"I asked him to visit because I knew he could help."

"I didn't realize you had extended a special invitation."

"Well," she hesitated, backing up, "it wasn't like that necessarily. I just thought it would be nice to see him. Isn't it?"

"Yes, but it's not like he's here every year. Was this your idea of good timing?"

"I guess you could say that. But you have to admit—we don't have many relatives like him."

"I wish I had an understatement bell. It would be a-ringing."

"You know what I mean. He came to Christ relatively late in life but has approached his faith with a fire that you don't often see. I think that's good for all of us. And I think we're a blessing to him too."

"And now I have to find a way to wrangle E, S, and T out of him before he goes home."

"He does have kind of a dramatic sense, doesn't he?"

"You think?"

Chris's phone came to life with a buzz on the dashboard. He still had it on silent mode from the board meeting. It was Sam Morgan.

"It's Sam again. I forgot to call him back from this afternoon."

"Strange that he'd call this late."

Chris took the call. "Hey, Sam. Sorry I didn't return your call earlier. It's been one of those days."

"I understand. Got a couple of minutes to talk now?"

It was the tone of voice, not grave but not jovial either. This was about to be a serious discussion. What had they found in the test? He needed to act cool so that Allie wouldn't pick up anything. No need to get her worrying. Chris determined to stay positive on his end, the end where Allie was sitting two feet from him.

"Sure—what's up?" he said, not really wanting to know.

"Got the results of your MRI. Your pain is coming from an injury to your thoracolumbar fascia, which is pretty general. But it's the load transfer area of your back, which is why you feel the pain moving, but can also get comfortable sitting still. It's not uncommon."

"Doesn't sound serious."

"Always like to treat any back injury carefully, but, no, we can get you through it."

Chris breathed a sigh of relief and remembered to smile for Allie's benefit. He turned to her, holding his hand over the phone. "Thoracolumbar fascia, dear," he said, as if he knew anything about what that was. "Don't think it's—"

"Chris," Sam interrupted. "There's, uh, something else. The MRI picked up a spot."

Everything slowed down.

He was certain his smile dimmed, because Allie turned immediately.

"The MRI seems to be picking up an abnormality in the region of the L-2 vertebrae, lower back. We don't think it's related to the injury, but we need to get a better look. The location has us a little concerned. I don't want you to panic; it could be absolutely nothing. But the smartest thing is to make sure it is nothing."

"I understand," Chris said, not understanding.

"Look, buddy, —you know I'm going to take care of you. But we both know the One who holds you in His hand."

On the next beat, Sam Morgan started praying. Chris wasn't hearing the words, but he knew they were the right ones. Allie reached over and put her hand on his knee.

Chris thought, *I'm yours, Father.* But he caught himself breathing, "What else?"

Four

FIGHTING THE FIGHT

● Chris, Allie, Amy, and Jake had many great memories of conversations around their kitchen table. It had become the primary gathering spot in their home, which frustrated Allie, because she tried to create other space where people would feel comfortable, but they always ended up at their old kitchen table, a wedding present she guessed would outlast them. Every scar or scratch in the wood was a reminder of building a family together. It was at this table that Allie was sitting when she got the call that she was pregnant with Amy, where Jake accepted Christ as a seven year-old, where they planned their cross-country vacation five years earlier. And now it was at this table, late on this Friday evening, that they prayed for Chris.

"Look, everyone—let's try not to get ahead of ourselves with this," Chris said. "Let's look this stressor square in the eye and not let it overtake us. Remember our R?" Even if everyone at the table could hear his heart beating, he knew that they would follow his lead.

"Dad," Amy asked, "are you afraid?"

Chris thought for a moment. "Well, I guess on some level, Sweetie, there *is* a temptation to fear. And I'm sure hoping this turns out to be nothing. But I think Uncle Ted's right. I need to be aware of how I'm responding to this and not let fear or anxiety take over."

"Exactly right," Ted said, still holding Allie's hand. "Mark says that in cases like this, the fear, the stress response, can cause more damage than the actual problem."

"But how do you just decide not to be afraid?" Jake asked.

"I think having feelings of fear is different from being afraid," Allie said, her strength more evident with each word. "It's a step of faith. As a family, tonight, right now, we are making a decision to trust God, despite what our emotions are telling us. Circumstance never trumps Providence," she said, quoting her husband.

"Our lives are in His hands anyway," Ted said. "No different right now than it was this morning or five years ago. When I gave my life to God, I said at that moment, *The rest is up to you, Lord.*"

"I've never had a time in my life that has been quite like this one, obviously." Chris added. "And it's been a roller coaster—that's for sure. But I really do believe God is in this. And while that doesn't make it any easier maybe, it's what I'm trusting in."

"It's what—it's *who* we're trusting in," Allie added.

"I'm not pretending it's not scary, putting up some kind of false front. I'm looking God in the face and telling Him I trust Him more than what I can see."

It was quiet for some time. Then Ted, who had been leafing through his Bible, began to read Psalm 23:

> The Lord is my shepherd, I lack nothing. He makes me lie down in green pastures, he leads me beside quiet waters, he refreshes my soul. He guides me along the right paths for his name's sake. Even though I walk through the darkest valley, I will fear no evil, for you are with me; your rod and your staff, they comfort me. You prepare a table before me in the presence of my enemies. You anoint my head with oil; my cup overflows. Surely your goodness and love will follow me all the days of my life, and I will dwell in the house of the Lord forever.

He drew a breath. "Now, is there anyone here who does not believe every word I just read?"

"I believe it," Jake said, speaking for everyone. "Is anyone else hungry?"

A chorus of rolling eyes.

"Honey, it's almost midnight," Allie said.

"Pip, he's a growing boy."

"I've had some of my best meals at midnight, I'll have you know," Ted said. "I could make donuts if you had a deep fryer."

"And I suppose you could make us a pizza if I had one of those giant ovens," Allie quipped.

"Don't ever joke about pizza, Missy," Ted said in mock seriousness. "Pizza is not to be trifled with."

Allie and Jake went to the kitchen, Allie undoubtedly to find a snack, Jake to make sure it wasn't too healthful.

Ted turned to Chris. "Get your notebook, son. I think this is a good time to introduce you to my friend E."

● ● ●

"I was wondering when you were going to get back around to REST," Chris said. "You do have a flair for the dramatic, don't you?"

"Everything has a season, my boy," Ted said. "Everything has a season."

"You only think that sounds wise. It doesn't."

"Look, do you want your E or don't you?"

"Okay. Let's have it. Although I thought I'd get a little more sympathy in my weakened condition."

"Oh, brother. Okay. Mark used to call E 'the opposites' of the REST tactic because it consists of the things we tend to avoid when stressed, yet those very things are some of the most important."

"If you're seeking to confuse me, mission accomplished."

"Just think about the things that you tend to want to do when you're under stress. The tendency is to crawl into a little ball, at least figuratively, isolated and still. You don't feel as much like being with people, right?"

"That's true. I've tried to lock myself in my office more lately."

"And I've noticed you haven't been exercising as much."

"Well, yes, but part of that is my back. But it's true that I've been less motivated."

"And then finally you'd like to be able to sleep, but you can't, right?"

"Also true. I haven't been sleeping."

"And those are the three elements of E—Engagement, Exercise, and Sleep. Mark talks some about diet here, too, but the focus is on those three."

"Sleep doesn't begin with an E, you know."

"Well aware of it, son. This isn't an exact science. But you get the point. E consists of the three things we really need to fight stress, but they tend to be those things that suffer when we're under stress."

"We need to be engaging with people."

"First with the Lord—it always starts with Him—and then with people. But we tend to try to isolate ourselves when we're under stress, especially heavy stress, like what you're experiencing. Spiritually, your enemy would love for you to seal yourself off from others during this time. Pun intended. Isolation is not your friend during this time. Actually, as a believer, isolation is never your friend."

"And everyone knows that exercise relieves stress."

"And it really does—not too many medical people question that. But when we're under stress, we're less motivated to head to the gym or get out and walk or get on a bike. We tend to do the opposite of what's good for us."

"And sleep?"

"That one took me a little by surprise, because I was always one of those people who didn't need much sleep. Four or five hours and I was good—didn't need eight."

"And?"

"And Mark is convinced that *everyone* needs seven to eight hours of sleep a night, even showed me some of the medical literature on it. Says there are numerous body functions—and especially brain functions—that need the time. Really important for fighting stress."

Chris checked his notes. "Engagement, exercise, and sleep."

"The 'E' of 'R-E-S-T'."

"Okay, but this is all easier said than done. What if I don't have time to engage?"

"You make time. This whole process is a conscious choice you make. That's one reason you can't *not* respond to stress, or it will take you over. Things like keeping God's Word moving in you, being involved in a church small group, planning time with friends, talking around the kitchen table late at night. Those things all matter."

"And exercise, with my back?"

"Exercise doesn't mean you have to be a triathlete. It means you have to move consistently, every day. You can walk, can't you?"

"In my condition? Where is your compassion?"

"Please. You get the point. You exercise the best you can. Most importantly, you figure out some way to move every day. Even if it's walking more or using stairs at work. I've fallen in love with this wall climbing thing at my gym."

"You would. And how do you sleep when you *can't* sleep?"

"Well, exercise and nutrition have a lot do to with that. But I've found some herbal supplements that help me sleep when I have trouble. Brought some with me if you would like to try them. Got a little white noise machine. That helps too."

Chris thought about the nightmares a man like Ted might have. What kind of memories from his time at the Hanoi Hilton POW camp might surface when he's drifting off to sleep? What level of heartbreak from planning the funerals of two beautiful wives would haunt his quiet? Chris had never experienced the feeling of wondering whether the airplane he was flying in was going to blow up under him. Yet Ted was enthusiastic, positive, content, joyful. It was obvious to Chris that this man was, first, a work of God, and second, a matter of REST. To look at Jake, mouth-full-of-cookie, and Allie and Amy's smiles, Ted had determined to make an impact for God in the people with whom he engaged. And he was a success.

"You really do know this stuff, don't you?"

"It's Mark's stuff, but it has been a tremendous blessing to me. Like I said—a godsend."

"Why do we tend to do the opposite of these things when we're feeling stressed?" asked Amy.

"Mark says it's fight-or-flight gone haywire. We have these God-designed defense systems that have to be disciplined, surrendered to Him; otherwise, they can be really destructive. They're there to protect us, but they get twisted, turned on and never turned off. Plus the fact that we're bombarded by external stimuli at every turn. Stressors everywhere you look—chronic stress."

"Did you just use the word 'stimuli'?" Chris asked. "And 'chronic'?"

"Hey, I'm way smarter than I look."

"I'm not sure that's possible, Uncle Ted," Amy said.

"One more reason why I love this girl."

"I'm going to pursue the part of 'E' that doesn't begin with E," said Allie. "My bed is calling."

"Night, all." Chris was the last to get up from the warmth of the table. As he turned out the lights, he reached his hand around to grip his lower back, wondering just how severely his world was about to be rocked.

●●●

If Chris ever doubted what kind of influence Sam Morgan had at their regional hospital, the fact that he got Chris in at 10:00 on the following Monday morning said all that needed to be said. The man could pull some strings. Chris had been scanned, poked, and prodded, and now he was waiting to meet with the lead neurologist. He was glad that Allie had a food bank advisory board meeting. She had wanted to cancel, but Chris thought it better for her to be occupied with something else. Besides, she still didn't seem to be feeling well herself.

He was told that they wanted a much closer examination of what had been detected on the MRI. It seemed as though every hospital staff member he talked to that morning mentioned specifically that if there were anything there, it was likely benign. "These things are usually nothing." Chris hadn't spoken with the janitor—he was unsure of his thoughts on the matter.

It had been a weekend of battle with Chris in the middle. He was determined to fight the good fight of faith, to trust God despite the apparent circumstances, and to apply the REST tactic as best he could, or at least R and E. Chris and Allie took advantage of the unseasonably warm weather and took a long walk together on Saturday morning. The conversation was encouraging, helping to ward off the sneaking dread. On Saturday afternoon Chris attended a function at St. Pio's and found himself in the corner of the auditorium chatting with the other vice presidents. They talked about the fact that at Wooten's previous school he had had more divisions and so more VPs than Mumphrey had had at St. Pio's. Perhaps he was considering adding executive staff without terminating any of them. Chris chuckled to himself, because while he had no business worrying at all, his future at St. Po's had now become only *second* on his list of things to worry about.

On Sunday morning he went back to the 1 Peter 5:7 text as the basis for his Sunday School teaching: "Cast all your anxiety on him because he cares for you," Chris read to the class and to himself. He had the feeling that God wasn't finished with that topic for his Sunday School class, and he was certain that God wasn't finished with it for him. He also referred to the Matthew 11:28-29 text. He read, "Come to me, all you who are weary and burdened, and I will give you rest. Take my yoke upon you and learn from me, for I am gentle and humble in heart, and you will find rest for your souls." Then the class talked about what it meant to be "weary" and "burdened" from a twenty-first-century context. Chris ended with a reference from Psalm 68:19-20: "Praise be to the Lord, to God our Savior, who daily bears our burdens. Selah. Our God is a God who saves; from the Sovereign LORD comes escape from death." That meant a great deal to him at that moment.

Chris wanted to teach the REST stress tactic as well. But he needed a clearer picture of the whole thing before he could feel qualified. He could always just stand Ted up in front of the class.

The board members he interacted with on Sunday spoke very positively about the board meeting and about the potential for Chris as the new lead pastor. He saw Peggy Sharpes only from a distance. No read there. The fact was, Chris cared whether the board members considered him a viable candidate for Kent's job. First, it would be problematic, to say the least, for Kent to prefer Chris against the wishes of the board, especially if the board decided to support one of the associate pastors. It could be messy. And second, Chris had to admit he wanted to be the solution. That didn't mean that he was certain he could or would take the job, but it did mean that he cared about the church. Beyond that, if he weren't considered a potential candidate, what was their next step?

If it were possible, Kent was preaching even more powerfully as his days at First Church grew fewer. Never known for his subtlety, he preached that morning on hearing the call of God. He might as well have called Chris's cell phone and just preached it that way. Chris smiled at the thought of the message as he mindlessly thumbed through a worn waiting room copy of a *Highlights* children's magazine. Gallant was helping an old lady across the street while Goofus threw mud on her. Those two.

A nurse appeared from the web of offices adjacent to the waiting room. "Dr. Seal?" Since she wasn't much older than his students, her addressing him with his academic title gave the scene a suddenly St. Pio's feel. She walked him back to the neurologist's office, not an examining room this time but an actual office. The place could most kindly be described as, well, a wreck. There appeared to be a book, chart, or file on every single surface in the room. There were plastic spines everywhere, which gave it a kind of toy store atmosphere. It was less an office and more a junk drawer.

The nurse gestured to a chair, but she didn't need to since it was the only surface where one could sit within twenty-five feet. Chris prayed that the doctor was like Columbo, a rumpled savant, a kind of slob-genius. He played with newly coined words "genlob" or "slenius." On the positive side, there were more degrees and certificates on the wall than Chris could count.

"Chris?" Just a normal doctor, no raincoat, entered the room. "Gray Anderson. Sam Morgan referred you to me."

Dr. Anderson was probably a little older than Chris, but his reddish-blond hair and freckles lopped off some years. He struck Chris right away as both very sharp and very warm. Dr. House meets Howdy Doody.

"First of all, I know this kind of thing can be a little scary. But, trust me—you're in the right place." He tapped some keys on his computer and turned the monitor toward Chris. "What we're looking at is this little thing." He used a pencil to point to a spot on Chris's spine, a tiny, poorly-formed grayish dot. Chris wouldn't have even noticed it if it didn't have a yellow pencil sticking out of it. "The good news is, your injury is going to be fine. You played college basketball, right?"

Chris was impressed.

"You'll be back on the court in no time—it's this thing we have to pay attention to," he said, pointing again. "The tumor."

Chris learned that that word has two different meanings, one when referring to someone else, a different one altogether when referring to you.

"Sometimes they grow out of a full-blown genetic disease like neurofibromatosis, tuberous sclerosis, something like that. Those can be serious, but that's not what we're looking at here. In fact, spinal tumors are relatively rare, but, as you can imagine, we take them seriously. So we're going to attack this one."

"Okay." Chris said, but he must have sounded hesitant.

"Chris," Anderson said, "I'm really good at this stuff. Trust me."

Tears warmed Chris's eyes.

"So, here's the deal. I'm going to go in, get a little piece of it and it won't be able to hide anymore. I can get at it with a needle so you'll be in and out. If it's something to be concerned about, I'll go after it with a vengeance. So let's get a biopsy scheduled."

Chris couldn't have explained it, but he just trusted the guy. He was one of those people who is so confident, so caring, that you just believe whatever he says. As Chris thanked him and navigated his way through the corridors to the exit, he heard a familiar voice:

"If you feel that way about someone you just met, how much more should you feel that way about *Me*?"

• • •

There was something about coming home that always gave Chris a sense of comfort. Allie had called him a homebody more than once, and he took it as a compliment. Pulling into the driveway, especially after this day, gave him a sense of peace, a peace that was about to be jostled.

Throwing his keys onto the kitchen table, he noticed two things: first, the fact that all was quiet and no one was in sight, yet Allie's car was in the driveway. *Well, they're somewhere,* he thought, not realizing the obviousness of that concept. The second thing he noticed was an envelope from Lawrence Marshall College. It was notably the only thing now, other than his keys, on the table, as if positioned there.

There was a story behind Lawrence Marshall College. Amy had dreamed of attending the prestigious school since she was thirteen or fourteen. Some kids aren't quite sure what they want to be, even at their college commencement. But Amy knew early on. She wanted to attend LMC for its nationally recognized pre-law program. Students with Marshall bachelor's degrees could choose virtually any law school in the country, and that was Amy's goal. They had spoken many times about her vision. "Like it or not, Dad," she would say, "lawyers get a voice in this country that some others don't have. And lawyers from the best schools can have the loudest voices. I want to be a voice for the gospel. I want to be someone who defends those who are defenseless." She spoke that way even as a high school freshman. Amy was passionate about the less fortunate, the marginalized in society. She had always made it a point in school to find the least popular lunch table and sit there.

She was an apple that hadn't fallen far from the Allie tree.

Amy was willing to work hard for her goals. She had taken high school seriously. She wasn't the kind of student who could coast on intellect alone. She had to work. And she did. Chris had seen her make many sacrifices because of what she sensed was the call of God on her life. They all admired her, even Jake, who didn't quite have her drive. And that is to say he cared just enough about school to survive it.

Against Chris's advice, Amy had applied to only one school, Lawrence Marshall. "I'm going to trust God, and if I don't get in— well, let's just cross that bridge when we come to it." It was an admirable step of faith, for sure, but a risk too. If she was waitlisted at Marshall or, even worse, rejected, she would be late applying to whatever school happened to be her backup. And she might be stuck.

And speaking of being stuck, there was something else—the cost. Lawrence Marshall was thirty-five thousand dollars a year. Chris winced just thinking about it. He had multiplied thirty-five times four many times in his head. The economy had virtually wiped out their college savings plans. They had a year, and that was about it. As a small college administrator, Chris wasn't wealthy. And what if that became a pastor's salary? Allie did most of her work *pro-bono,* which is Latin for "public good"—which is English for "you can't afford Lawrence Marshall College." Amy could probably borrow the money, but Chris had known many students of his own who graduated from college under a mountain of debt, so much so that graduation wasn't a very happy time. Chris didn't want that for Amy.

Nonetheless, this was his daughter's dream, and he refused to root against it just because he didn't know how he would make it happen. *The fact that I think I have to make it happen is my first problem.*

He picked up the envelope. *You, my little friend, are a stressor,* he thought. *I will make godly choices about how I respond to you. I will recognize the potential for negative stress here.* Usually a small envelope meant a rejection, while a large packet was an acceptance. However, more and more schools, including St. Pio's, were sending letters in either case, with acceptance letters providing a link to a password-protected website containing the acceptance information. So the size of the envelope really didn't answer any questions for him.

The envelope had already been opened neatly with a letter opener creating a slit at the top. Then it had been carefully folded, returned to the envelope, and placed on the table. *Allie and Amy, partners in crime.*

He slowly removed the letter and read, "We're pleased . . . " and that's when the screaming started.

The three of them had been hiding in the family room, "lurking," he would later call it, waiting for him to read the wonderful news. But seconds after he reached into the envelope, they could no longer contain themselves. They hopped up and down and screamed their way into the kitchen, almost knocking Chris over. He felt a rush of joy, seeing the light in his daughter's eyes. Her work had paid off. Amy Kathleen Seal was going to be a freshman at Lawrence Marshall College.

She was on her way.

That thought slowed him down, as she transformed from an eighteen-year-old hopping up and down to a four-year-old praying in her beautiful little voice for God to "bless the peoples and the pusghetti." Or to a ten-year-old confronting a neighborhood bully, or a seventeen-year-old off to her junior prom. And that was the kicker. Chris slumped into his chair and began to sob—beautiful, glorious tears of sadness, joy, and gratitude. That, of course, had Allie and Amy crying and Jake slipping out of the room.

They talked about her plans for orientation in the summer and for the move. Marshall was a six-hour drive south. There was much to do. Chris refused to allow his concerns about the money ruin this moment. But they were there. He had no idea how this would work, but he knew it had to.

He heard Ted's rental car pull up into the driveway, and he thought of E.

"Let's take a walk," he said to Allie.

"Before dinner?"

"Sure. Just get your coat."

"OK. That's good because," she sing-songed, "I know something you don't know."

Chris wasn't sure his life could fit anything else.

•••

It was chilly, but not cold, as the winter warming streak continued. Their neighborhood had remnants of the most recent snowfall. Although plows had pushed snow against the curb, there was still room to walk on the sides of the street and very little traffic at this time of day. Things were quiet. Chris and Allie walked without saying anything. They had already spoken by phone more than once about his meeting with Dr. Anderson. He had described the doctor, the office, and the spot in as much detail as he could. They read each other well enough to know that neither wanted to talk about it anymore today.

Allie eventually broke the silence. "Do you believe she did it?"

"As a matter of fact, I do. What a girl! Just like her mom."

Allie laughed and squeezed his hand.

"You're worried about the money, right?" It wasn't as if they hadn't spoken about it many times before.

"You know, it *is* an issue, but I'm thinking it's time for me to walk my talk."

"What do you mean? You always walk—"

84

"I mean I've been telling others to cast their burdens on the Lord. That's exactly what I'm going to do. I'm not going to give worry and anxiety an opening."

"Oh, yes—R. Good choice. I just can't get out of my head how many times in our marriage we've been in a position where we just had to trust God. And it's not always what we're expecting, but He's always there. It's as Kent says: 'People will probably let you down—Jesus never will.'"

He knew she was exactly right. He also knew that there would always be just a little hesitancy involved in being a person of faith, since believing was the substance of things *unseen*. It was trusting God without letting what might happen darken what is happening. Kent had cited a paraphrase of Matthew 6:34 that Chris remembered: *Give your entire attention to what God is doing right now, and don't get worked up about what may or may not happen tomorrow. God will help you deal with whatever hard things come up when the time comes* (TM).

"Okay, what's up?" he asked.

"What do you mean?"

He mock sang, "I know something you don't know." putting his arm around her.

"Oh, yes. Well, I have a little surprise."

"All ears over here."

Their neighbor, Carl Nicks, was coming the other way walking his St. Bernard, Mr. Duferton. Carl didn't seem to be that happy about it. Mr. Duferton did. They exchanged greetings with Carl and were gleefully slobbered on by his dog. Mr. Duferton was a people person; Carl, not so much.

"S," Allie said.

"S?"

"I know the S in R-E-S-T. Uncle Ted told me while we were painting the Food Bank today."

"No way!"

"Way!"

"Well, let's hear it. But remember: I don't have my legal pad with me, so you're going to have to repeat some later."

"S is 'Say thanks.'"

"Okay, so R is recognize stressors as they're happening to you and realize that those things are normal. Avoid the 'freak-out' factor."

"And E is engage, exercise, and sleep."

"The latter of which does not begin with an E."

"Amen. And S is "say thanks," which he describes in three parts."

"Go with part one."

"Part one is an attitude of gratitude. Instead of having this tunnel-vision focus on everything that's wrong, everything you want God to fix right now, be grateful for what you have been given. 'Remind your mind'—that's his term—about the good God has done, the blessings in your life. Force yourself to think of the good, even when you're seemingly surrounded by bad. The text is from Philippians 4:8."

"I've taught about an attitude of gratitude."

"I remember."

"But I can't say I've ever thought of it as a stress management tool."

"The idea is that so much of how you manage stress is happening in your mind, both in terms of the way your brain is actually functioning during times of stress and how your heart is responding to that."

"Check. Part two?"

"Part two is an emphasis on the word 'say' in 'say thanks.' He says that it's important not just to *feel* gratitude but to *demonstrate* it too. When you are grateful, say, 'Thank you;' when you love someone, tell him or her. Don't keep your gratitude a secret. Don't assume those around you know how you feel. 'Saying thanks' means *saying* thanks."

As they turned the corner for their house, Chris could see through the large front window that Ted had the apron on, speaking of serving. The man just attacked life, like Mr. Duferton on a ham hock.

"And part three?"

"Part three is to get your attention off yourself and onto others. God, family, friends, others. The S under the broader heading of 'say thanks' is 'serve.'"

"I'm starting to get the theme here. Narcissism is like gas on the fire where stress is concerned."

"That's right. Uncle Ted told me the story of Sharon's death. He said he was just locked into grief for the longest time until he started helping another widower move. He said the woman who had passed away had a house packed with trinkets and knick-knacks. He and this gentleman spent two weeks sorting through all the stuff. When it was done, Uncle Ted knew he was in a better place—something about the power of bearing another's burdens."

"And I'm guessing cataloging five-hundred figurines was quite a sacrifice for him."

She smiled.

"Okay. S. I'm on it. Maintain an attitude of gratitude. Don't just *be* thankful—*say* thanks. Look for opportunities to serve others and invest your time in that."

"Perfect."

"I have some questions, of course, but I'll save those for the man himself." He gestured to the window. "Has he asked you for any new kitchen appliances lately?"

"He said it was a travesty that we didn't have a garlic press."

"He actually used the word 'travesty'?"

"Travesty."

They stopped at the driveway and looked together at their home. The sky was full of yellows and purples now, and they were just about out of daylight. The orange light coming from the front window gave the house a soft glow against the spectacular backdrop. She rested his hand on his lower back and whispered something he couldn't hear. Amy was on her cell phone smiling and holding up her precious letter. Somewhere Mr. Duferton barked playfully at something.

"What are you thinking?" she asked.

"What I'm thinking is in two parts."

"Go with part one."

"Part one. I'm so grateful for you, Pip. I don't even want to think about what my life would have been without you."

She smiled and lowered her head into his shoulder.

"Part two. I love you."

Five

REST-ING

● Chris woke up thinking about the old gag: *When did you first realize you had a weak back? Oh, about a week back.*

He chuckled to no one in particular. Yes, he knew it wasn't that funny. The irony was that his back was feeling as strong as it had since he fell. There was much less stiffness and hardly any pain. Not being an expert on tumors or spots or "the c-word," he didn't know if that was a good sign or more a calm-before-the-storm. He did remember his *S* and started by running through a list of everything he was grateful for—or at least everything at the top of his head. He said aloud, "Lord, I'm paying attention to what you are doing right now, and I will not get worked up about what may or may not happen tomorrow. I know you're already there anyway." He made a point of thanking God specifically for that day. That one day.

It would be a full day. Dr. Anderson was doing the biopsy first thing. They would at least know what they were dealing with within forty-eight hours, he said. He also warned Chris that there might be some discomfort.

"And by discomfort, I mean pain."

"So, can I plan anything for the rest of the day, or am I going to be flat on my back recovering from this thing?" It was the first real medical issue Chris had ever experienced, other than getting his tonsils out when he was twelve or the occasional sprained ankle.

Having been a high school and college athlete, he had gotten good at taking care of himself and hadn't experienced much sickness. He really had no idea what he was dealing with. No amount of Googling gave him a clear picture.

"No, you won't be flat on your back. In fact, it's probably good to stay off your back and keep your mind occupied. Move." (Did he know Uncle Ted?) "Just no mountain climbing, shot putting, or uneven parallel bars."

Why did doctors always see themselves as closet comedians?

Chris had asked, because the follow-up board meeting was scheduled for that night. He didn't want to delay either the biopsy or the meeting; that meant they ended up being on the same day.

He wanted to warm up the car for Allie, since she was driving him and still wasn't quite ready. He pulled on his coat and headed out the front door. He smiled, seeing Kent sitting in the driveway in his car with the motor running. His Bible was propped up on the steering wheel, and a cup of coffee was in his hand.

"What are you doing here?" Chris said as Kent lowered his window.

"Oh, do you live here? What a coincidence! I just happened to be in the neighborhood."

"Do you really think it's appropriate for a man of the cloth to lie?" They both laughed.

"Today is a big day for you. so I wanted you to know I'm with you; more importantly, so is He." He lifted his Bible.

"You worried about the board meeting?" Chris said.

"I can honestly say I'm not worried about a thing. I'm in trust gear. Trust Him with the church, trust Him with my life, trust Him with yours. Besides, what's happening this morning is a lot more important than what's happening tonight. How you feeling?"

"Okay, I think. I'm starting to handle all this in a much more God-aligned way."

"So I hear. When you get a chance, you need to tell me more about this REST thing."

Ted appeared at the front door. "Chris, don't leave yet—I made you a couple of biscuits." He was holding up a brown paper bag. Aunt Bee on steroids. He'd been up for hours already. "Oh, hey, Pastor Kent. Want something to eat?"

"No, thanks, Ted—got my coffee."

"I got eggs!" he said as if announcing he'd just won a sweepstakes.

"Thanks, anyway." Then back to Chris. "Hey, if it won't weird you out too much, I'm just going to follow you to the hospital before I head off to a meeting."

"You don't have to—"

"Nope, don't have to—I get to."

On her way past Ted and out the front door, Allie grabbed the paper bag but couldn't escape one of Ted's giant hugs. "Praying for you guys today!" he called to Chris.

The procedure was done in no time, literally no time from Chris's perspective. They had set him up in a kind of pre-op room, with just a curtain separating him and his embarrassingly backless hospital gown from a bustling hallway of doctors, nurses, patients, and visitors. Dr. Anderson appeared through the curtain, described the procedure, and left to prepare. Chris was wheeled to the procedure room, greeted by the two nurses there, and put to sleep. Once he watched the drugs drip into his IV, all he remembered was singing to himself, *This is the day that the Lord has made. I will rejoice and be glad in it . . .*

As far as he knew, he was back in the pre-op room in a minute, but it was actually about an hour. He did remember waking up and recalled the first thing he said.

"Pip?"

"Right here. How are you feeling?"

"Groggy." The clearer his head got, the more pain he felt, hot, sharp. "Does hurt some."

"They gave you some medicine for that." She was standing beside the bed, holding his hand, with her other hand resting on the top of his head.

His mind wandered, and despite all he was learning, worried. He found himself thinking about all he was losing. He was losing a friend and pastor. Kent would be far away in just a few weeks. He was losing Amy; she would be far away in just a few months. Would he lose his job? The church? Briefly he allowed, "Am I going to lose my life?" to flash. He cracked his eyes. The bright green readout at his bedside showed his vital signs. His pulse and blood pressure were rising right in front of him. He was doing this to himself.

Then he stopped.

No. Cast your cares.

Yes. You have a lot to worry about. It's all on you.

No. Come to me, all you who are weary and burdened.

A scene-scape filled his mind. Was he dreaming? Three crosses on a hill, purple-orange sky, people scattered all around, all eyes on a slumped, thorn-adorned head. Chris whispered, "Thank you." And maybe Allie interpreted that as a thanks to her, because she drew close. And it was, partly. But it was first a thank-you to God for all He had given Chris, not the least of which was the woman by his side. He thought of Amy, Jake, Ted, the church. But bigger, God-on-a-cross, forgiveness, mercy, life—a shower of blessings he couldn't start to count.

Life.

Allie saw a grin grow on his face.

• • •

Knowing that there was nothing he could do about the results of the biopsy was a strangely comforting feeling. He knew whose hands it was in. He had been released from the hospital by noon and actually felt good enough to go to lunch with Allie. The medication they had given him for his pain was doing its work with no notice- able side effects. It was strange that three hours after a cancer biopsy, although everyone was careful not to call it that, he was choosing between jalapeño poppers and mozzarella sticks with Jimmy Buf- fet playing in the background. Dr. Anderson was a get-out-of-the- hospital-and-get-on-with-your-life kind of guy. Chris loved that.

No matter—this lunch was for his girl.

"Well, tonight's the night," she said.

"Before we get into that, let's talk about you."

"Well," she said cocking her head, "I like men of God, baby kit- tens, and long walks on the beach . . ."

"I bet you think that never gets old."

"That's because it never does," she said with a crafty smile.

"You know what I mean. Over these last few weeks it seems as though everything has been about me. I'm tired of everything be- ing about me, and I want to pursue S and focus on you. It's a stress management tactic."

"That's clever. Right now, it *is* about you, Chris. There have been lots of times over the past when I was the focus. It's a give and take. You know—the whole marriage thing."

"Pip, something's been going on with you. Are you saying that it's all been my stuff?"

"Sweetheart, do you remember when I was involved in that tough case trying to protect that sixteen year-old mom and her daughter?"

"The Carly Casullo thing? Sure."

"How many hours did you spend talking me through that, praying for me, staying up late with me?"

"But that's just part of the deal, Pip."

"The defense rests, your honor."

"Oh, you're good. You're very good."

"Let's get through this season, and I'll dump all my stuff on you. Until then, I'm holding up your arms."

"So it isn't all my stuff then."

"Is that Peggy Sharpes?"

Chris turned to see Peggy walking, actually marching, toward their booth with two men Chris assumed were business associates. He was sure that Peggy loved God, but there were times when she could be scary. Now was one of those times.

"Chris! Allie!" She waved her associates on to a table somewhere beyond them. Was it too late to throw themselves under the table? Cover themselves in jalapeño poppers camouflage style?

"Pastor Chris Seal—I have a bone to pick with you! I just found out what you've been going through with your back and your tests, and you didn't say a thing!" It was an odd combination of compassion and frustration.

There were about ten different things to which he could respond. Why was she calling him "Pastor?" How did she find out about his tests? Was she planning to hurt him? "Peggy, I—"

"Look, I know I'm not always the most sensitive person. But not only are we family in God's eyes—there's a good chance you're my next pastor, at least if I have anything to do about it. I haven't just admired you from a distance; I care about you and your family."

Chris and Allie looked at Peggy and at each other with their mouths politely agape.

"You know, I know people at the hospital. How are they treating you? If there's anything you need, don't let money be an issue. It's on me. Who's your doctor?"

"I—"

"It should be Gray Anderson. If it's spine, it should be him. No one better."

"That means a lot. Everything's good so far. In fact, I just came from the biopsy."

"Father, I lift up your boy here." Peggy had put her arm around him and grabbed Allie's hand. She was praying in the middle of the restaurant, loudly enough that Chris was sure people at the adjacent tables were going to be healed. "I pray you would speak clearly to him about becoming our pastor, and I ask you to heal him completely and absolutely in Jesus' name. Amen. See you tonight. Big board meeting."

Then she kissed him on the head. Peggy Sharpes kissed him on the head. Kissed him. On the head. And she was gone.

Chris and Allie stared at each other. He touched his hair where Peggy had kissed it, as if there might be a moon rock up there. Since someone had to speak, he did. "What just happened?"

"Well, it's clear we've been transported into a parallel universe of some sort."

He looked around the restaurant, souls in the middle of their days, smiling, maybe hiding hurts no one knows. "You know what this is about?"

"Love to know."

"This is about S."

"Say thanks? How?"

"Remember the S is about getting your attention off yourself and focusing on others."

"Peggy."

"Sure. Think about what she's been through, the loss she's experienced, and how often she's had to trust God. Desperately."

"And how she's processing Kent's leaving and the potential of a new pastor."

"Exactly. It's time for me to start paying attention to how others are processing all of this and what I can do to serve *them* rather than having such an inward focus. What's going to happen to *me*—how *I'm* affected."

"Do nothing out of selfish ambition or vain conceit. Rather, in humility value others better than yourselves," she said, recalling the Philippians 2 text, "not looking to your own interests but each of you to the interests of the others.

"In your relationships with one another, have the same mindset as Christ Jesus: Who, being in very nature God, did not consider equality with God something to be used to his own advantage; rather, he made himself nothing by taking the very nature of a servant, being made in human likeness. And being found in appearance as a man, he humbled himself by becoming obedient to death—even death on a cross!"

As he said it, his eyes caught Peggy's. Lowering her water glass, she slowly smiled.

Maybe the board meeting wouldn't be quite what he was dreading.

Either Chris was learning how to deal with stress, or the drugs were working, because he felt his shoulders relax as Allie reached out and took his hand.

•••

Ted referred to dinner that night as "the last supper" with a maniacal laugh. Chris told him that he didn't find it funny yet caught himself laughing. The biopsy, the encounter with Peggy, and now the prospect of that evening's board meeting made this a day that

Chris and Allie would likely never forget. On top of it all, Dr. Wooten had phoned Chris that afternoon from an out-of-town conference where he was the keynote speaker. The primary reason for his call was to check on Chris, which meant a lot to him. But Wooten had mentioned having a "brainstorm" at the conference and wanting to meet with Chris the following day, if he was up to it. Chris wasn't sure if the brainstorm was a new opportunity for Chris or a way to phase him out gracefully. It might just be moot.

"You know what it's time for?" Ted announced professorially from the kitchen.

Chris could only guess. "Cake? Cookies? Figgy pudding?"

"Well, first of all, figgy pudding is a very under-appreciated dish, but that's not what I'm talking about."

"What's it time for?"

"T."

Chris had pages of legal pad filled up with notes on R, E, and S. Recognize stressors and realize they are normal. Engage, exercise, and sleep. Say thanks. He had been so busy taking apart the first three concepts that he hadn't spent much time wondering about T. He knew enough now to know that both medically and scripturally, Ted's friend and doctor, Mark Huddleston, was on to something about a God-aligned response to stress. While he knew that nothing as complex as stress could be oversimplified into a simple four letters, he also knew that before the REST tactic he hadn't even thought about his responses to stress and how harmful they could be if he didn't start to think differently. REST was a start, and a good one. He had begun to study key people in the Bible. Chris couldn't find any that didn't have significant stressors, some on the level of life and death. Abraham, Moses, Joshua, David, Esther, Debra, Peter, Matthew—a seemingly endless list of men and women facing threat, conflict, frustration, broken relationships, self-doubt, fear.

Chris had also spent time studying Jesus, especially in light of the incredible stress of Passion Week. He didn't have all the answers, but he had learned that what Ted had said was true. Stress couldn't be something he simply allowed to happen to him without an active response. If he didn't respond, it could have a destructive impact relationally, emotionally, physically, and spiritually.

"Yeah, it's about time for complete REST."

"Are you waiting for a drum roll?" Chris called.

"Think differently—trust God," Ted said, coming in wiping his hands on a dish towel.

"So it's two Ts."

"We've been through this before; it's not an exact science."

"Just sayin'. Which order?"

"Mark uses 'trust God' first. I use 'think differently.' He says too many people see a call to trust God as an over-simplistic platitude."

"First of all, I'm just impressed that you use the term 'over-simplistic platitude.'"

"Who uses that term?" Allie said, joining the fray from the family room.

"I may be twice your age, but I think I can still take you, young man," Ted said in mock anger.

"Well, you're not twice my age, first of all. Just get back to trusting God."

"It's easy to tell someone to trust God. That can be a pat answer to every problem in life."

"Well, it *is* the answer, isn't it?" Allie offered. "I've heard Kent say, 'Unbelief is the root of uneasiness.'"

"Sure, but when someone, like your boy here, is in the middle of a tough situation, dealing with some life-altering, gut-wrenching stuff, he needs real counsel, real encouragement, not just a catchy slogan. So in the end, trusting God is the key to genuine contentment, joy, and peace. It's the ultimate stress management tactic. But it's easier said than done. It requires a new way of thinking."

"The two go hand in hand?"

"Yes. If you can't get to a place where you trust God, you will battle fear, anxiety, unrest, stress. One way to approach that is by thinking differently, literally changing your mind. It's Romans 12:2—"Do not conform to the pattern of this world, but be transformed by the renewing of your mind. Then you will be able to test and approve what God's will is—his good, pleasing and perfect will." So if you want to test and experience 'good' 'pleasing' and 'perfect,' it requires a change of mind. Think differently."

"Are you talking about Bible study, prayer, worship—those kinds of things?" Allie asked.

"Absolutely. But not just those things, although all are critical, the wings of the aircraft. It's also about seeing things differently. For instance, a lot of times we divide our lives into what's sacred and what's secular."

"Compartmentalize."

"Yep. But when you're following God, it's *all* His. You don't put on your work hat to go to the office and then take that off and put on your super-spiritual hat to go to church. Every step, every circumstance is ordered by the Lord. When you give yourself to God, it's *all* His—family, work, church, hobbies, vacations, biopsies."

"What's the impact on stress?" Chris asked scribbling on his legal pad.

"Think of it this way. When I first became a Christian, I remember I got this bumper sticker that said, 'God is my co-pilot.' I know my heart was in the right place, but I had it all wrong. If God is only in the right seat, He's in the *wrong* seat. He needs to be driving! If we think of our lives as the God part, the sacred, and then separate from that is the non-God part, the secular, we're on our own for over half our day! *We're* doing the driving."

"Or at least we think that way," said Amy. Apparently she wasn't so focused on her homework.

"Yes, my dear. And that creates a negative stress response. Mark says sometimes it's subconscious, but either way, we need to change that thinking. God is in all of it—every detail of our lives. There is no 'sacred versus secular' for the believer."

"Think differently—trust God," Chris said.

"I like it in that order," Allie said. "A lot of the time, going from fear to trust is first a change of mind for me."

"Whatever works for you, my dear. The whole sacred-secular thing is just one example."

"We need to get ready to go to the board meeting. So Ted, will you be stalking us out in the hallway again tonight?"

He feigned ignorance. "Why, I wouldn't know what you're talking about."

"I bet you wouldn't. You know you can pray just as well from here."

"I think those drugs they're giving you are making you a bit loopy."

"Yeah, I'm experiencing loopy all right," Chris said, gesturing to Ted. "Or are you Sneezy?"

The drive to the church for the board meeting was lighter than Chris was expecting. His back was more than sore, and he couldn't help wonder what the tests would reveal. But there was much less fear than he had expected. He knew he was experiencing what the Bible calls "peace that passes understanding," and he was grateful for it. He didn't know what the board meeting would hold, but he knew that he was making a decision, now more than ever, to trust the God who made him.

●●●

In the conversations that Kent and Chris had since the last meeting, Kent was supremely confident. He reminded Chris that hearing from God was in his pastor's job description and that he invested much time in learning the voice of the Lord. He didn't believe in Chris just because he liked and admired him, but he believed in him because God had chosen him to lead First Church. As a result, he expressed zero misgivings about that meeting. In fact, Kent had already begun to speak about how the transition would work. Confidence? Probably more trust.

So when Peggy Sharpes smiled broadly at Chris as she was seated, perhaps that was all that needed to happen. Even Scott Hampton had made a point of encouraging him as they were chatting before the meeting started. If everyone knew that this meeting could be a dark day in the history of the church, they weren't letting on. This was a difficult decision, and if unity couldn't be achieved in the room, there would be big problems. And there was Chris, in the center of it all. *But this isn't about me.* Then he prayed, *Lord, let me be absolutely the last person I think about tonight. Oh, and Lord,* you *drive.*

Kent turned and winked at Chris. Then Dr. Daniels opened the meeting. "Thank you all again so much for being willing to invest in this process. I know there's been a great deal of prayer and fasting over this past week. There's no doubt in my mind that we have given this to God, and He has responded. Who would like to start?"

Scott Hampton was quick to his feet. "Since I was pretty vocal last time, maybe it should be me."

"No." Chris stood and approached them. He wanted to look at each board member closely. "Excuse me, Scott, but if you'll allow it, I'd like to start."

Scott breathed a loud sigh of relief and took his seat.

"I've learned a lot over these past few weeks. I've been walking with the Lord for some time now, so it's a little frustrating to realize I still haven't learned it all. I guess I haven't 'arrived' yet."

"Join the club," someone said.

"But I was wrong to make this all about me and whether *I* was called, or *I* could do the job, or *I* could replace Kent, or what was going to happen to *me*. That's not the call of Christ on my life, and it's certainly not the way we do church. It's about what *He* wants, first, and how I can be a servant to you and to this family. I've been creating all the stress in me and the people I love because I've been worried about planning, succeeding, being qualified, what could go wrong, what disaster might happen in the future, measuring up. I've acted as if God wouldn't be in my future, in our future, when in fact He's already there. Since this was a difficult process, I took it as strange, as if God couldn't be in the hard stuff. That made the problem even worse. I've wanted to isolate rather than engage. I was worried more about being trustworthy in my own strength than trusting in His strength first.

"Preach it!"

"So, I'm here to tell you that Allie and I have prayed. I would be honored to serve you as the next lead pastor of First Church—honored." There. He said it. It was a decision he and Allie had made together, a few days after the last meeting. He had to get clear of the negative stress response before he could truly hear God and obey Him. Until he started learning to handle the stress, his emotions were obstacles. But once he had started the process, praying with his Bible and trusty legal pad in front of him, he was surprised at how quickly the path cleared.

After his announcement, Chris was expecting a somber and thoughtful discussion to follow. He was thinking someone would break down the pros and cons. He was thinking there might be multiple layers of voting. Then it got so loud he wasn't able to think anymore.

There were cheers and whistles and hoots as the board members rose to their feet to gather around Chris and Allie, who was by his side. Even Chris knew unity when he saw it. *Good thing I was really worried about all this,* he chided himself. God had been at work. It was only theirs to trust Him.

Each board member took turns hugging him and shaking his hand. All offered words of encouragement.

"I was afraid I would scare you off when I got all slobbery" was Peggy's first comment. "Whatever you need—" But she couldn't finish through tears.

After the unanimous "Amen" vote, there were loose ends to tie up. Actually, they were more than loose ends. There would be a congregational vote. The board members seemed confident that the church family would embrace Chris, who started to feel a dull ache in his stomach at the thought of it. But right on time, Dr. Daniels offered a prayer that God would bring the congregation comfort in losing the pastor they loved and unity in accepting their new leader.

No one was thinking that the transition would be easy, especially Chris and Allie. You don't lose a pastor like Kent Wallace seamlessly. The goodbye party for Kent and Angela would be full of mixed emotions, no doubt. But at the heart of it was a trust that God was ordering things. *Trust and obey, for there's no other way . . .* was the old hymn that Kent had started them singing.

For Chris there was the finality that set in. He was leaving St. Pio's, a place that had been his home. He could be transitioning from a regular guy to a cancer patient in a matter of hours. He was happy, but it wasn't a happy ending in the sense that all was neatly sewn and sealed. Still, *Give your attention to what God is doing right now, and don't get worked up about what may or may not happen tomorrow. God will help you deal with whatever hard things come up when the time comes.*

• • •

Executive vice president.

That was Wooten's brainstorm. At their meeting that morning, Wooten shared that he did want to replace Chris with one of his VPs from his previous school, in fact one who had visited. But he didn't need three weeks to know that he wanted Chris to be part of St. Pio's well into the future.

"I want to promote you to EVP, and I don't want to wait," Wooten said. "You would be senior over all the vice presidents and serve as my chief of staff. So you would have significantly more responsibility and a modest pay increase. Sorry it can't be more. No vice presidents will lose their jobs, although we need to have a conversation about changes for a couple. Of course, you would lead the search for the new provost."

It took a beat to sink in. It was strange that he would be handing in his resignation a moment after being offered a promotion. In fact, the irony of the whole situation must have played on Wooten as well, who continued to eye the envelope Chris was holding.

He wasn't going to lose his job after all. He would have been promoted had he stayed. *Good thing I was really worried about all this.*

"Dr. Wooten, I'm very grateful that you would consider me. And I want to make it clear that I love St. Pio's."

"Chris, I think you have a 'but' coming here, don't you?"

"I do. I apologize for springing this, but I thought I had a few more weeks."

"That's my fault. I told you it would be longer, but I had a colleague remind me at the conference that you don't make a star wait three weeks."

"That's very humbling. But I want you to know that I've made the decision to leave St. Pio's." He stopped. "Actually, that's wrong. I haven't made the decision to leave here—I've made the decision to accept God's call to be the lead pastor at First Church."

It was clear that both of their worlds were rocked at this moment. For a beat, neither knew exactly what to say next. Students were crossing campus past Mary-Theresa Kennedy's statue. A faculty member Chris knew was taking photographs. *I really am going to miss this place.*

"Well, if I have to lose you, what better place to lose you to? If you feel as though your decision is final, could we talk about how I might continue to have you involved here?"

Chris agreed to be available to serve on a part-time basis to consult with Wooten and to continue to teach adjunct. He wouldn't be leaving St. Po's altogether. In fact, Wooten's willingness to keep him on part-time would mean that Chris's transition would not result in a cut in pay overall, which he had initially estimated based on the church's pay scale. In fact, he would actually end up making a little *more*. God's hand in that wasn't lost on him.

The news wasn't as good from Dr. Anderson.

"First, let me give you the bad news," he said on a phone call late that afternoon. "It *is* cancer. And I know that's a scary word, but these types of primary tumors are rare and slow-growing. Osteosarcoma. You're a little older than normal for this type. Your fall and subsequent back injury actually helped you here, because we found it very early—a stroke of luck." Chris knew luck had nothing to do with it. "It's really small and about as far from myelin as it can get, which is good."

"Do you—"

Dr. Anderson anticipated the question. He had obviously been through this many times. "Okay, let me just say that, yes, you are going to die, probably drag racing at the age of 86. But not from this. I'm going to get in there and get it out. My neuropathologist says she doubts it's metastasized from anywhere else. Not the type. It's not impinging on any nerve function. We'll see about radiation or chemotherapy after I get in there." Gray Anderson knew how to tell someone he has cancer. "Chris?"

"Yeah, doc?"

"I got this."

Chris, Allie, Ted, Amy, and Jake all let the tears flow that night. But Chris found himself much less afraid than he thought he might. By now he had learned something about how to respond to these kinds of serious stressors. He wasn't kidding himself; he knew that cancer is cancer. But what was the best choice—anxiety or trust? *I can panic, fear, and allow stress to wreak havoc on my mind and spirit, probably growing the tumor, or I can realize this is the kind of trouble Jesus talked about, that it's part of life, engage with the people around me, take care of myself, focus on others with a heart of gratitude, and trust God. All things considered, I'm choosing REST.*

Several days after the successful surgery, Chris and Allie were lying in bed on a Saturday morning. He was staring at the ceiling and going over the next day's Sunday School class in his mind. He was teaching on E.

Under the covers, Allie grabbed his hand and turned to him. "Okay. Now can we talk?"

EPILOGUE

● Joshua Theodore Seal was born seven and a half months after Chris's surgery. Nine pounds, four ounces. "A whopper," Ted said, bouncing him up and down. Pastor Chris Seal's third child would unexpectedly return him to diapers and car seats and kindergarten and untold joy. They agreed early on that they would never, ever, refer to him as an "oops baby." They knew better. Allie had suspected but was hesitant to tell Chris until she was sure, especially considering all that he was going through.

The church had welcomed their new pastor warmly, although saying goodbye to Kent was as difficult as they expected. Kent didn't regret the move. In fact, Angela's mother had shown some improvement having the family there. Kent agreed to fill Chris's pulpit once every seven or eight weeks, and the two of them did some consulting work together for St. Pio's, where Chris stayed involved, developing a strong friendship with Dan Wooten, who was now a proud member of First Church.

Amy left home, and Chris survived it. She loved Lawrence Marshall, as she knew she would. She diligently pursued several scholarships, which helped with the finances significantly. She was faithful to call and to Skype, which was a big help to Chris. It also helped that his hands were full with JT and that Jake was still, well, Jake.

Ted stayed through Chris's surgery, always the rock, and, of course, visited again just before the baby was due. Chris later learned that Allie had arranged Ted's visit when she first suspected that she might be expecting. She had no idea what would transpire and how desperately Ted would be needed. Someone did, though.

Gray Anderson calls Chris a cancer survivor, because he is. The surgery went perfectly, and no further treatment was needed. "Let's see each other once every six months for a while." Chris agreed to the deal, but only if Gray agreed to clean his office.

Chris's life did not become "stressor-free." No one's is. But he did learn to think about REST and to fall more deeply in love with the only One who could truly grant it.

Section 2

THE MODEL

Six

THE STORY OF STRESS

Do not fear, for I am with you; do not be dismayed,
for I am your God. I will strengthen you and help you;
I will uphold you with my righteous right hand.
—Isaiah 41:10

● Tom Hartman is a pastor of a church of three hundred or so in the Midwest. Tom felt called to the ministry early on, but lately he's not so sure. His congregation expects him to do just about all the ministry. The factions in the church are constantly pulling at him. At the upcoming board meeting he expects an argument about something that the college youth leader said from the pulpit. But it won't be a surprise, because there's always an argument about something.

Tom is tired. He told a pastor friend last week that he now knows what burnout is. The friend told him to get used to it. He is often just plain angry, but, of course, he can't show it. After all, he *is* a pastor. He's gotten quite good at faking it. The pressure is impacting his marriage. Food helps, though. The problem is that Tom has gained twenty pounds in the last three months.

●●●

Cynthia just celebrated the one-year anniversary of her divorce from her ex-husband. He wants virtually no part of their three young children and often cancels his scheduled visitation. When she was in the failing marriage, she let herself dream about the relief that the single life would bring. Freedom. The problem is that there is never a minute to enjoy whatever freedom she tells herself that she has. She loves her three children—seven, five, and three—but she has found herself lately thinking of them as a burden. Her migraines have increased both in frequency and intensity. She doesn't want out, but she wants rest, just a break, a weekend to herself. It never ends. A glass of wine after the kids go to bed each night has turned into three.

• • •

Carla and Ronnie are in that season. Both thirty, their lives revolve around their children. Emily is four, and Charles is seven months. Ronnie is trying to build a career and volunteer at church as best he can. Carla just craves sleep. She admits that she has thought about ignoring Charles's cries at three AM, and she feels terrible about it. Carla and Ronnie don't really talk in the evening anymore; they just kind of collapse together. Romance is sneaking the kids to bed early and falling asleep in front of the television. They don't want this life, but that's the sacrifice it takes to raise a family. They are both sick more often than they used to be, but they chalk that up to having kids. Ronnie has found some release sitting at his computer late at night.

• • •

Jason has been under-employed for three years now. He was a six-figure software engineer, but the company he worked for downsized and never re-sized. He's heard from old friends that the company is just barely getting by, even now. Jason gave up on the chances of getting called back a long time ago. He works at a local office supply store making about a third of what he once made. Every time he puts on that red shirt with his name on it, he feels the same sense of embarrassment. Jason is deeply in debt and can see no way out.

He used to pray, but it doesn't seem to work. He is now accustomed to the sick feeling in his stomach. It's his constant companion. He doesn't really sleep anymore. Oh, he gets *to* sleep because he has a doctor who has been willing to refill a prescription more times than he should, but it's not real, refreshing sleep. Jason doesn't allow himself to hope.

• • •

What's your story? It's probably not precisely the story of Chris Seal or even one of these examples. But if you bought a book about stress and have read this far, you want some answers. And you're not alone. The American Institute of Stress describes the stress epidemic.

> Numerous surveys confirm that adult Americans perceive they are under much more stress than a decade or two ago. A 1996 *Prevention* magazine survey found that almost seventy-five percent feel they have "great stress" one day a week with one out of three indicating they feel this way more than twice a week. . . . It has been estimated that seventy-five to ninety percent of all visits to primary care physicians are for stress-related problems.[1]

If you're working at understanding and combating the negative effects of stress in your life, you're on your way. A significant first step in dealing with stress, or more specifically the destructive capability of chronic stress, is looking it squarely in the eye and determining to do something about it with God's help.

What stressors cause negative responses in you? A relationship? Your career or lack thereof? Your boss? Your church? Your bank account? Everyone faces stressors, those things that create a stress response. That response can be a healthy, God-designed approach to handling the trouble of this world, or it can be destructive—wearing out, overusing, or overriding the protective systems with which you were God-formed. It's probably hurting you more deeply than you may realize. It certainly isn't part of God's design for your life.

DESIGN

Stress. There are many definitions and approaches to the word. One researcher considers trying to place an all-encompassing definition on *stress* to be a "futile exercise."[2] Of course, while it is a very complex concept, physically, spiritually, and emotionally, and while it is beyond the purpose of this book to peel off all its layers, we must come to some understanding of what we mean by the word. Andrew Bernstein in his book *The Myth of Stress* cites the definition from the *American Heritage Dictionary* as typical of our understanding.

> Stress: A mentally or emotionally disruptive or upsetting condition occurring in response to adverse external influences and capable of affecting physical health, usually characterized by increased heart rate, a rise in blood pressure, muscular tension, irritability, and depression.[3]

Bernstein's problem with this standard definition involves the term "adverse external influences." His argument is that there is essentially no such thing as an "adverse external influence," because whether something is "adverse" or not is not found in the stressor but in us. It is based on how we think.[4] The thing itself isn't adverse, but how we perceive or think about it makes it so.

We have a different problem with the standard definition. Our problem is that it doesn't address the design, purposes, or power of God, the central issues in a believer's life. It also doesn't address the destructive power of sin and its relationship to stress.

But let's start at the beginning. If you ever doubt that you are "fearfully and wonderfully made" (Psalm 139:14) in the very "image of God" (Genesis 1:27), spend some time studying how your brain works.

Your brain is a miracle.

The brain is so complex that it may not be able to figure itself out. You have a mind designed to handle everything, from loving God with passion to instantly steering to avoid a child running into the street to chase a ball. At our church we saw the powerful story of a mother who, with her son, lifted a car off her husband after it had fallen off a jack and pinned him under it. It broke her back and saved his life. Like her, you are wired to overcome, and that is even more important in a world as uneasy as ours.

You are the reflection of meticulous design, created with intention down to each individual cell for exactly what you need at each moment. You truly are wondrous. Walter B. Cannon, who is considered one of the pioneers of the study of stress, entitled his seminal book *The Wisdom of the Body*.[5]

If you'll forgive a science lesson, it starts with the processes of homeostasis and, more specifically, allostasis,[6] essentially your brain's work at making sure that all systems are go in your body for the specific situation. The idea is that, for instance, the blood pressure you need for your morning devotions is different from what you need for your third mile on the treadmill. Robert Sapolsky in his book *Why Zebras Don't Get Ulcers* concludes, "A stressor can be defined as anything that throws your body out of allostatic balance—for example, an injury, an illness, subjection to great heat or cold. The stress response, in turn, is your body's attempt to restore balance."[7]

The culprit in all of this is your autonomic nervous system in general[8] and adrenaline and cortisol specifically.[9] When you are faced with a stressful situation—the child running out into the street in front of you, your suddenly screaming toddler in the backyard, a spider where a spider shouldn't be, a note that your boss wants to see you—the hypothalamus in your brain springs into action. Your adrenal gland, located near your kidneys, produces adrenaline, which quickens your heart rate and elevates your blood pressure. Cortisol, the main stress hormone, increases the sugars in your blood to make quick energy available to your muscles, increases your brain's efficiency in using glucose, and makes ready your body to repair tissues. Cortisol also makes sure that your energies are devoted to all of the fight-or-flight activities that your body will need in the moment and not so much the ones it won't, the latter including your immune system, digestion, reproduction, and growth.[10] You don't really need to be worrying about fighting disease or digesting that calzone when fending off a barking dog, teeth bared, ready to take a chunk out of you and your bike.

Of course, once the threat is gone, your body's God-planned systems return again to allostasis, all systems normal for the current situation. The production of adrenaline and cortisol stops, and you can get back to work on that calzone. Peace and tranquility. At least, that's the idea.

And that brings us to our problem.

What if it doesn't stop? What if the way you approach your life keeps your body in stress mode far more often than you were designed for? This is referred to as *chronic stress*. It has wide-ranging negative effects. Researcher Mary Carmichael concludes that it impacts not just our body's ability to respond but also our brain's.

> In humans, almost anything can start the stress response. Battling traffic, planning a party, losing a job, even gaining a job—all may get the stress hormones flowing as freely as being attacked by a predator does. Even the prospect of future change can set off our alarms. We think, therefore we worry. Herein lies a problem. A lot of us tend to flip the stress-hormone switch to "on" and leave it there. At some point, the neurons get tired of being primed, and positive effects become negative ones. . . . Neurons shrivel and stop communicating with each other,

and brain tissue shrinks in the hippocampus and prefrontal cortex, which play roles in learning, memory, and rational thought. "Acutely, stress helps us remember some things better," says neuroendocrinologist Bruce McEwen of Rockefeller University. "Chronically, it makes us worse at remembering other things, and it impairs our mental flexibility."[11]

Your brain is so well designed that it responds not just to an actual danger, the enraged German Shepherd chasing your Schwinn, but also to *perceived* or *expected* dangers as well. Fear, worry, and anxiety create a stress response in us, the same stress response as when the danger is real. Fear is a response to stress and creates more of it.

You've probably heard some pastor at some point mention that "Fear not" is the most frequent caution in the Bible. In your own study of the Word, you may have noticed how often people are encouraged to "be strong and courageous." When you read in Isaiah 41:10, "Do not fear, for I am with you; do not be dismayed, for I am your God. I will strengthen you and help you; I will uphold you with my righteous right hand," the study of stress dictates that you take that very seriously. When Peter tells you to "Cast all your anxiety on him because he cares for you" (1 Peter 5:7), consider a literal interpretation. As you begin to learn about how we stress ourselves out, it becomes clear that those biblical entreaties really are for our own benefit.

Sapolsky's conclusion is "When we sit around and worry about stressful things, we turn on the same physiological responses—but they are potentially a disaster when provoked chronically."[12] The system that was hard-wired into us when we were formed in the womb (Psalm 139:13) is designed to "respond to acute physical emergencies, but we turn it on for months on end worrying about mortgages, relationships, and promotions."[13]

For example, you'll recall that one of the ways in which cortisol is so effective is that it depresses the work of your immune system. In the heat of a high-stress moment, your body, in effect, takes energy from the immune system and uses it for more important, in-the-moment activities. It makes sense, then, that chronic stress, the overproduction of cortisol through worry and fear over anticipated danger, has the impact of suppressing your immune system to a point at which disease, which might not normally impact you, can make you sick.[14] But that's just one of the possible negative results of chronic stress. Sapolsky notes,

> In kids, growth can be inhibited to the point of a rare but recognized pediatric endocrine disorder—stress dwarfism—and in adults, repair and remodeling of bone and other tissues can be disrupted. If you are constantly under stress, a variety of reproductive disorders may ensue. In females, menstrual cycles can become irregular or cease entirely; in males, sperm count and testosterone levels may decline. In both sexes, interest in sexual behavior decreases.[15]

The Mayo Clinic adds to the list of potential problems created by "long-term activation of the stress response system . . . heart disease, sleep problems, digestive problems, depression, obesity, memory impairment, skin conditions."[16] Stress can even age you before your time.[17]

The web site <livestrong.com> cites the American Institute of Stress in listing the top ten causes of stress. They are—

1. Childhood trauma
2. Death of a loved one
3. Divorce
4. Finances
5. Job
6. Health
7. Personal relationships

8. A chronically ill child

9. Pregnancy

10. Danger[18]

Which of those are impacting you? And we mean you, specifically and individually, because you were created uniquely. What causes an unhealthy stress response in you is not the same as that in someone else. Moreover, it's likely a combination of things that may be working on you. That's what it was for Chris. He didn't consider himself someone who was normally *stressed out*. But there are many factors and seasons that play a role in determining how you will respond to the stressors in your life. And that response is at the heart of things.

For us, stress is a mind-body-soul state in which, through mistrust, worry, and fear, we alter the design and purpose of God for our lives, putting us at risk of spiritual, emotional, psychological, and physical harm. Does that mean to be stressed is to sin? We'll discuss this in more detail later, but be sure: sin is by definition destructive (Romans 5:12, 6:23; Hebrews 3:13)[19]. Unconfessed sin creates negative stress; it can't be "managed" in a safe way. Many have tried. When considering the source of stress in your life, please start there. You can't be free from stress until you are free from sin.

• •

Consider

The 1 Peter text referenced throughout this book calls you to "cast all your anxiety" on God. Proverbs 12:25 adds that "anxiety weighs down the heart."

What are you anxious about? What fears or worries trigger a stress response in you? What concerns send your cortisol into action when it isn't really needed?

Make a list. We're talking about actually sitting down and writing a list on paper. Finally, next to each stressor write key words that describe the feelings that each one seems to evoke in you. How does the stressor make you feel?

How intense are those feelings? This relates to what is often referred to as your self-talk and is a very powerful factor in how you respond to stress.

Where you begin to see fear-related words—*worried, anxious, afraid, concerned, panic,* and so on—marks the starting point. Walk through your list with someone you love and trust— spouse, pastor, close friend—and ask that person to pray with you about the list. Admit to God that you haven't done such a good job handling these things so far and that you need Him. Tell Him out loud that you are casting these things to Him. Then throw the list away. Don't put it on the refrigerator or write it in your Bible. Just get rid of it, both literally and symbolically. If any of those things knock at your door again, cast them again. If you need help, get help through your church or a Bible-based counseling center.

You don't have to live in chronic stress.

Seven

REST
RECOGNIZE STRESSORS AND
REALIZE THEY ARE NORMAL

The mind governed by the Spirit is life and peace.
—Romans 8:6

● "It's all in your mind."

You may have heard that said before as if to claim that something isn't real. And sometimes it isn't. If you're afraid you have cancer but you don't really have it, it really is all in your mind. It isn't real in that sense. If you fear losing your job and the fact is that you are not at risk of losing your job, that fear is all in your mind. It isn't true.

Stress is immune to that argument, however. With stress, it *is* all in your mind, and it *is* very real. For instance, if you're afraid you have cancer but you don't, the cancer may not be real, but the fear is, and it can have a very real harmful effect on you. Your stress response doesn't know the difference between cancer that is real and the fear of cancer. It doesn't know the difference between actual bankruptcy and anticipated bankruptcy.[1]

While we don't necessarily agree with Bernstein's recommended steps to deal with pressure in *The Myth of Stress,* we do think his conclusions about the origins of stress are helpful:

Stress doesn't come from what's going on in your life—it comes from *your thoughts about* what's going on in your life. Your job isn't stressful—*your thoughts about* your job are stressful. Your relationship doesn't stress you out—*your thoughts about* your relationship stress you out. All stress is an inside job, a result of subconscious assumptions.[2]

Every life has stressors. Every single human being will face events that will call a stress response into action. That's why God designed the stress response in the first place. You're not the only person with an imperfect marriage or challenging children. You're not the only person who has experienced too much month at the end of a paycheck or not enough forgiveness by the people in your life. That doesn't mean that our stressors aren't important. Of course they are. They are important to us; otherwise, we wouldn't bother with this book. And they are certainly important to God.

But the problem of stress is not found in the stressors themselves; we too often think that's the case. The problem of stress arises from our *response* to those events or people. "A central assertion of the Theory of Preventive Stress Management is that stimuli in and of themselves do not generate individual outcomes. Rather, the outcomes resulting from stressors are mediated by the response of the individual to those stressors."[3]

This implies a choice. Things will happen in your life—hard things. Your level of stress stems from your response to those things. This may have been what Jesus was getting at in John 16:33 when He declared, "In this world you will have trouble." That's something you already know. But this choice we're talking about may be reflected when you expand that text. "In this world you will have trouble. *But take heart!*" (emphasis added). That means you. "I have overcome the world." The reason Jesus taught this message? "I have told you these things, so that in me you may have peace."

So you have trouble. *And* you take heart, if you choose.

Take heart.

First, recognize stressors and their potential to harm you. Work to understand the power of your attitude in determining whether you will have a healthy response or not.

If you don't like where you are right now in terms of how you are experiencing stress, start with Paul's instruction to "be transformed by the renewing of your mind" (Romans 12:2).[4] Stress is not something that can be approached passively, as if allowing it to take the path of least resistance is somehow God's way. "Do not fear" and "Be strong and courageous" are commands to make choices—active, thoughtful choices.

Further, if we become obsessed with our problems, we worsen the stress by becoming anxious *about our anxiety!* In scientific terms, the way a person thinks about the stress he or she is under can impact the level of stress. What you *believe* about your stress also matters. Sapolsky concluded that the way we feel about our stress, what we believe about it, and more specifically, the level of control we feel we have makes a difference.

> Place two people in adjoining rooms, and expose them both to intermittent noxious, loud noises; the person who has a button and believes that pressing it decreases the likelihood of more noise is less hypertensive. In one variant of the experiment, subjects with the button who did not bother to press it did just as well as those who actually pressed the button. Thus, the exercise of control is not critical; rather, the belief that you have it.[5]

Fear of death can be a major stressor. For some, it's number one. Paul thought about it when he was in prison. Imminent death was very real to Paul in that Philippian jail. He made an active choice about how to respond to that stressor. He made a decision to think differently about the potential to fear death. In *The Message* paraphrase he describes his thoughts.

On the contrary, everything happening to me in this jail only serves to make Christ more accurately known, regardless of whether I live or die. They didn't shut me up; they gave me a pulpit! Alive, I'm Christ's messenger; dead, I'm his bounty. Life versus even more life! I can't lose. As long as I'm alive in this body, there is good work for me to do. If I had to choose right now, I hardly know which I'd choose. Hard choice! The desire to break camp here and be with Christ is powerful. Some days I can think of nothing better. But most days, because of what you are going through, I am sure that it's better for me to stick it out here. So I plan to be around awhile, companion to you as your growth and joy in this life of trusting God continues. You can start looking forward to a great reunion when I come visit you again. We'll be praising Christ, enjoying each other (*Philippians 1:20-26*, TM).

I (Brian) once had a fairly serious health scare. I was afraid, experiencing a gripping fear for perhaps the first time in my life that I was going to die. I know I was experiencing deep anxiety and what some would call "panic attacks." During what was probably my lowest period in this death valley season, a friend looked me in the eyes and said, "Tell God you're movin' on." I wasn't exactly certain what he meant. He gripped my arm firmly and said, "This is what you say to God: 'Father, either take me to heaven or let me live my life, but I will not be afraid. I'm movin' on.'" At first it sounded a little cold. But he was exactly right. I said that to the Lord, and I believe it honored Him. I started to think differently about what I was going through. (Since it was fifteen years ago, it's clear that He is faithful, and I really did move on.)

How can you follow Paul's model in thinking differently about your fears? Right now you may be thinking one way. You may be worried, afraid, anxious. Those feelings may be the result of destructive, chronic stress and may be producing more of the same. Even if you aren't necessarily sensing stress on an emotional level, you may have read enough to be convinced that cortisol is running free and wild within you. But it doesn't have to be that way. Paul knew that. You can too. If you've been following Christ for long, you probably have suspected that believing matters. After all, "without faith it is impossible to please God" (Hebrews 11:6). So it should follow that faith is central to the way you think about what is stressing you. Faith isn't just the cornerstone of *saving* your life (Romans 10:9); it's the way of *living* your life (2 Corinthians 5:7). "The life I now live in the body, I live by faith in the Son of God, who loved me and gave himself for me" (Galatians 2:20).

Once you have it, stop thinking.

Seriously. Often the problem is not just the quality of our thinking but the quantity as well. We become transfixed by our problems, running them over and over again in our heads. That creates more stress and compounds the problem. There comes a time when it's counterproductive to continue thinking and talking about what's troubling you.[6] That's one reason that focusing on others, which we will discuss later, is such an important part of dealing with stress.

Next, understand that stressors are part of life. Don't be alarmed when the things in your world aren't running as smoothly as you think they should be. If you want a twisted sense of encouragement, do a character study of key figures in Scripture. You name a man or woman in biblical history, and we can pinpoint a time when life wasn't what that person hoped it would be. Stressors? Try Adam. One of his sons murdered another one of his sons. Abraham? Climbing a mountain to kill his only son. You want to talk about stressors—how about Joseph? Sold into slavery by his brothers. Moses? Running for his life from a murder charge. Ruth? Faced with the prospect of leaving her mother-in-law, whom she loved. David? Fasting and praying that the baby he fathered in adultery wouldn't die. Mary? Endured the death of her brother Lazarus. Peter? Stared straight into Jesus' eyes after denying him. In fact, it's difficult to find a significant person in biblical history who *didn't* face hardship, just like you.

And there's more. As you look back on your life, wouldn't you admit that the strongest blessings and deepest growth came from your most difficult times? It's ironic, then, that when stressors appear in our lives, we still have the tendency to try to find a way around them rather than trusting that "Christ in us" (Colossians 1:27) really is our guarantee, our hope, through our darkest hours.

STRESS AND SIN

Think about how you would respond if you began to believe you were going to be laid off from your job. That is certainly a stressor. You may choose a reaction to that perceived threat in which you imagine a set of future circumstances wherein God is absent or His promises fail. You're on your own. When that happens, stress happens, crafting destructive responses manifested by worry, anxiety, foreboding, and dread. When that happens, one effect is that the promises of God become perverted in you, whether subconsciously or not.

"I know the plans I have for you," which the Lord declares in Jeremiah 29:11, becomes *I don't have plans for you; you're on your own, and you won't make it.*

"The Lord is my light and my salvation—whom shall I fear?" from Psalm 27:1 becomes *I am darkened and doomed; whom* shouldn't *I fear?*

"Do not fear their threats; do not be frightened," from 1 Peter 3:14, becomes *Be afraid. Be very afraid.*

You get the idea.

You may argue that fear is an acceptable response. "Isn't it perfectly normal," you might counter, "to worry about job loss, the effects of a bad economy, the health of a spouse, the state of your church, or any other serious situation? I mean, these are reasonable reasons to stress, right?"

To put it succinctly: *wrong.*

What's normal is the presence of the stressor, not the accompanying fear, worry, and anxiety. Those responses are abnormal as far as God is concerned. If you've put your trust in Christ and committed to follow Him, fear is not only not normal—not just a poor response to stress—but by God's measurement it is sin. At its core, fear is the opposite of faith.

It is a reaction that empowers stress to hurt you.

When Jesus and His men were in a boat crossing the Sea of Galilee, a storm arose that caused panic to take root. These men were not normally timid, but this storm was something they viewed as a significant threat to their lives, and fear gripped them. You know, of course, that Jesus did not respond to this stressor in the way that His disciples did.[7]

He was asleep.

They woke Him, accusing Him of a lack of compassion for their plight, as if they considered it "abnormal" for Him not to be as afraid as they were. He rose, calmed the storm, and asked them a question about their fear. "Why are you so afraid? Do you still have no faith?" (Mark 4:40).

No faith? Is that what fear represents to the Lord?

Seems to be a somewhat stern (pun intended) comment considering the circumstances. But Jesus did not entertain fear as we sometimes do. Perhaps this is why without faith it is impossible to please God. Or maybe why the admonition "Don't be afraid," or some similar challenge, appears so many times in the Scriptures.

· ·

Consider

Read Philippians 4:4-7 in as many versions as you can find. The New International Version reads,

> Rejoice in the Lord always. I will say it again: Rejoice! Let your gentleness be evident to all. The Lord is near. Do not be anxious about anything, but in everything, by prayer and petition, with thanksgiving, present your requests to God. And the peace of God, which transcends all understanding, will guard your hearts and your minds in Christ Jesus.

Do you believe the promises there? If you do, make this a memory verse. Don't continue reading until you have committed the text to memory. Then do exactly what it says. Make it a theme verse for you for the foreseeable future.

If you don't believe it, be honest. Tell God. That's right—read Philippians 4:4-7 to Him aloud, and tell Him that you're sorry, but you don't believe it. You believe He exists—if you do—but you feel your life is too hard or your perception is that His promises have failed you. Tell Him you don't have His peace, and you don't see any way it even exists for you. Confess that to Him. Be honest with Him. Don't worry—you're not committing some kind of heresy, just being honest in the same way that the boy's father in Mark 9:24 was honest. Ask Him to help you believe. Tell Him you want to believe. Chances are, even if your head doesn't, your heart does.

And let us encourage you. It's all true!

REST
ENGAGE, EXERCISE, SLEEP

Above all, love each other deeply,
because love covers over a multitude of sins.
—1 Peter 4:8

● Attack.

When I (Brian) was growing up, we had a dog named Sully. He was a great dog, although, to put it mildly, he lacked the poise and polish of some of your finer dogs. I would call him a mongrel, but that would be a slight to mongrels everywhere. He was a mix of some of the worst of several breeds. Not cute, fast, sleek, or stylish—the Ford Escort of dogs. But he loved life. He relished his days, ran everywhere he could, and attacked the most mundane chore with vigor. He loved to build piles of rocks and then move the piles from one place to another. Our vet once warned us that if Sully wasn't careful he would wear his teeth down to nubs. Once when my mother was making a fine dinner for the birthday of a friend, he ate every bit off the table when we left the house to shout "surprise" as the friend was arriving. We walked in to find him standing on the table, smiling and belching. My mother uttered the kind of noises at that moment that, since then, I've only heard only in science fiction movies.

When it was time for a walk, Sully would drink in everything, as if experiencing the world for the first time. His head was always up, he was always trotting, ready for what was around the next corner, willing to save the world. He survived being hit by a car, relished a move of five hundred miles, loved other animals, loved people, and adored me. He was the ugliest hero I've ever known.

He lived life in attack mode without ever hurting a soul. The future was an adventure, defeats were simply forgotten, weaknesses not even considered.

When it comes to the second step in the REST model, Sully's idea is the right one. Take the offensive. Attack.

There is a kind of paradox involved in following "E." This step calls for you to pursue those things that are sometimes very difficult when you're suffering from the effects of chronic stress. We challenge you to engage with people, yet you might be tempted to go off by yourself when feeling stressed. We counsel you to exercise as a critical stress management technique, yet you will often feel completely unmotivated when dealing with anxiety or fear. Finally, we ask you to make sleep a priority, yet there may be times when you would love to sleep but instead lie awake for hours running your problems through your mind. The more difficulty you have sleeping, the more you feel the negative effects of stress. The more you're feeling those effects, the more difficult it is to sleep.

Chronic stress tends to fool us into behaving in ways that are the exact opposite of what is right, healthy, and godly. *Time* magazine reported that to be the case.

A November survey by the advocacy group Mental Health America found that we frequently deal with chronic stress by watching television, skipping exercise, and foregoing healthy foods. The problem with these coping mechanisms is that they keep you from doing things that help buffer your stress load—

like exercising or relaxing with friends or family—or add greater stress to your body.[1]

That's why attacking may be the best approach to pursuing E. Take the offensive, and make strong decisions that counter the negative effects of stress.

First, connection always starts with your relationship with the Lord. You can't build meaningful relationships with people if you aren't in a meaningful relationship with God. Take the initiative. Seek Him. That starts with a regular pursuit of His Word and mutual commitment to a local church grounded in biblical teaching and true New Testament community. It branches off from there and is reflected in the books you read, the music you choose, the prayer you invest, and so on.

Next, meaningful connection with people—sometimes referred to "social support" or "protective relationships" in the stress literature—is critical for reducing the negative effects of stress.[2] As it turns out, the people who love you are good for you. Surround yourself with them. All it takes is one. Look for opportunities to share community. Plug in as deeply as you can to that strong Bible-faithful church we mentioned above. If you don't have such a church, find one. Avoid the temptation to isolate.

The more connection, the better. People with spouses or close friends live longer. People who are socially isolated are more likely to have high blood pressure.[3] This was a finding in Sapolsky's research for *Why Zebras Don't Get Ulcers.*

> The fewer the social relationships a person has, the shorter the life expectancy, and the worse the impact of various infectious diseases. Medically, protective relationships can take the form of marriage, contact with friends and extended family, church membership, or other group affiliations. . . . Going

through a divorce or having severed marital problems—is also associated with worse immune functioning.[4]

As part of our research for this book, we asked a Christian counselor friend what is the single greatest enemy to the believer. We thought it would be helpful to hear the thoughts of someone who has advised hundreds of men and women facing the darkest of circumstances. He is a credentialed counselor who has been in the trenches for almost twenty years. We guessed that he would respond by saying that there isn't really one thing plaguing believers today but a series. We thought we might get a list. Instead, he answered immediately and with one word: *isolation*. His conclusion was that the greatest threat to the believer, and perhaps the most powerful weapon of your enemy, is to separate you out, get you alone, or thinking you're alone, so that you retreat in your pain. Once there, loneliness is allowed to feed on itself and despair to darken.

When we're suffering anxiety and depression, we tend to want to be isolated. We wallow.

It's understandable. It's very dangerous.

Peter's encouragement to love one another *deeply* (1 Peter 4:8) presents the antidote. You would think that it is enough to suggest that people simply love each other. That's a strong exhortation in and of itself. But adding that Greek word *ektenes*—translated here as "deeply"—creates the image of, literally, a "stretched-out" kind of love, covering the breadth of a life, its highs and lows.[5] To be loved so thoroughly by another is the true act of a disciple. For Jesus, it was the way others would be able to identify His followers.[6] And that helps explain why the New Testament in particular is so interested in community, the fellowship of believers, the power of love.

"You must love one another" (John 13:34).

"Be devoted to one another in love" (Romans 12:10).

"Let no debt remain outstanding, except the continuing debt to love one another" (Romans 13:8).

"Let us consider how we may spur one another on toward love and good deeds" (Hebrews 10:24).

Love acts. Just take a long look at that center cross.

Love has an impact on people. The best place for you when stress is threatening to tear you apart is to grab hold of a community of faith and don't let go. Find friends, a small group, and most of all a church that follows Christ as if their lives depended on Him.

EXERCISE

To say that exercise is a great weapon against chronic stress is to state the obvious. Do a Boolean Internet search for "exercise" and "stress," and you get 148,000,000 hits. So we won't belabor the point here. Exercise is an important weapon in your attack of stress.[7] Montes and Kravits studied exhaustive research conducted by the United States Department of Health and Human Services and concluded that "the findings show with universal consistency that exercise interventions decrease stress levels and increase feelings of well-being."[8] The chances are you already know that. But you also may think that in order for exercise to do any good you have to become a triathlete or a participant in one of those refrigerator-carrying contests, which actually exist. In reality, it doesn't take much exercise to do yourself a lot of good. The idea is to move as often during the day as you can. It might mean you get up and walk around every once in a while if your work life is normally sedentary. Take the stairs rather than the elevator.

Anyone who knows me (Kerry) knows that my philosophy of life includes this statement: Victorious living is mainly about the blood of Jesus, not the sweat of Kerry. However, I cannot overemphasize how essential riding bicycles with my wife, Kim, four or five times a week is as it pertains to returning me to real rest in an uneasy world. It works wonders.

For you, exercise might start with something as simple as watching less television. Researchers at the University of Vermont conducted a study of what happens to people when they watch less television. They connected monitoring equipment and tracked the habits of thirty-six men and women who were overweight or obese. When the experiment started, the people in the study were right about at the national average, watching five hours of television each day. In the experiment, about half the people had their television-watching cut in half. The result wasn't that those whose television-watching was reduced became highly-buffed professional athletes, but they moved more and behaved in ways that were healthier. In summarizing the study, the *New York Times* concluded that those with reduced television time ended up walking an average of eight miles more per week, even though they didn't necessarily plan to walk or take walks. The reduction of their television time simply had the effect of making them more active.[9] Moreover, television is a remarkably unhealthy and sedentary activity. One of the doctors involved in the study concluded, "Compared to watching television, you burn more calories reading, writing, doing desk work—pretty much any activity other than sleeping."[10]

We recommend starting with God first and your doctor second. Commit your desire to exercise to the Lord. Ask Him specifically to help you, to motivate you and to remove distractions. One way you can exercise and grow in intimacy with the Lord is to get a good audio Bible and listen to that while you're exercising, no matter what form the actual exercise takes. Next, have a good conversation with your medical professional about how you can work more exercise into your life. Then determine simply to move more. Don't set lofty goals that are unreasonable. It's unlikely that you're going to be able to go from zero to mountain climbing. Set goals you can achieve easily at first. You can increase them later. You might also want to engage an exercise buddy, which has been shown to improve a person's success at fulfilling exercise plans.[11] There are plenty of resources available to help you move more and stress less.[12] And exercise provides many benefits, beyond just helping you to fight stress. People who exercise tend to feel better, think more positively, and sleep more soundly.

SLEEP

Sleep is a great weapon against the negative effects of stress.[13] People who are experiencing chronic stress sleep less.[14] You can see the problems proposed by those two statements. If you are suffering from stress, sleep helps you, but you are also less likely to be able to sleep. If you've ever had insomnia because you were stressed about needing sleep, you know how frustrating the whole thing can be.

First, your sleep is something that God cares about. You're not on your own just because you've turned out the lights. You can almost feel the relief in the psalmist, who breathes, "I will lie down and sleep, for you alone, Lord, make me dwell in safety" (Psalm 4:8). Or David, who even when he was on the run, proclaimed, "I lie down and sleep; I wake again, because the Lord sustains me. I will not fear though tens of thousands assail me on every side" (Psalm 3:5-6).

Much has been written and researched on how much sleep you're supposed to have. While it's difficult to pinpoint exactly how much sleep any individual should be getting, researchers agree that chronic short sleep duration, defined in the literature as four to five hours or less, is associated with a wide variety of problems from poor school performance to insulin resistance to high blood pressure to obesity. Beyond that, it appears there is a "sweet spot" when it comes to sleep for adults. In other words, there is not enough sleep, and there is too much sleep. One recent research project summarized twenty-three studies conducted over the past thirty years and concluded that the seven-to-eight-hour sleep duration is about right. The risks associated with less than that are similar to those related to sleeping nine hours or more. Michael Bonnet and Donna Arand conducted research for the National Sleep Foundation, reporting, "Compared with individuals with a seven-to-eight-hour sleep duration, there is an increased risk of dying in individuals who reported a short sleep duration—usually substantially less than seven hours—and in individuals who have reported a long sleep duration—generally nine hours or more."[15] Many researchers agree that your body will help guide you concerning how much sleep you need.

The best news is that, yes, a good night's sleep can help you be less stressed and, yes, you don't have to deal with insomnia. There are techniques to help improve your ability to sleep. Exercise is a significant help, going to bed and waking up at a consistent time, waiting until you're tired before you go to bed—for those who have trouble falling asleep and so on.[16] Some have also had success with supplements such as melatonin or talking with their doctor about prescription options. One author suggests counting your blessings rather than counting sheep.[17] On the other hand, alcohol, caffeine, and smoking are major enemies of a good night's sleep. Avoid them.

Consider

Keep a journal for two weeks with a specific focus on how much time during a typical day you spend in meaningful connection with people. Meaningful connection usually means either having a substantive conversation or engaging in an activity, such as worshiping, praying, studying the Bible, playing a game, and so on. You may be surprised to learn that you don't spend as much time engaging as you think you do. That lack of engagement may be adding to your stress level.

After the two weeks are up, create a plan for the next thirty days in which you set a goal to increase your level of engagement. If you are not in a church-based small group, one great way to engage is to join one. At our church we often refer to it as "doing life together." Chances are, you will have to decide that you are going to spend less time in front of the television and less time meandering the Internet. That doesn't mean that those two pursuits are necessarily evil, but at the very least they are not helping you reduce your negative responses to stress, and at most they are making stress worse. The greater your connection to God and to others, the less likely you are to be stressed out.

Nine

REST
SAY THANKS

Let the message of Christ dwell among you richly as you
teach and admonish one another with all wisdom through
psalms, hymns, and songs from the Spirit,
singing to God with gratitude in your hearts.
—Colossians 3:16

● You see it every Christmas.

There's this guy who is surrounded by people who love him in a place he calls home. But he's stressed. And the more stressed he gets, the more blind he becomes, blind to the smiles, deaf to "I love you." Rather than seeing the good that's right in front of him, he sees his problems. He focuses on one particularly serious problem. He gets angry and lashes out. Finally, the pressure builds to such an extent that he decides to kill himself. It's the ultimate negative stress response.

That's when God intervenes.

The miracle that God gives him is not the birth of a child, healing from cancer, or even the solutions to his problems. The miracle God gives George Bailey is the gift of gratitude, the ability to see, clearly see, the blessings all around him. How does He do it? He takes them away, or at least He shows him a life in which he doesn't exist. In one scene George climbs the stairs, grabbing a loose post cap, which comes off, as it always does. He looks at the hunk of wood as though it were the source of all of his problems, the focus of all of his hate. He loathes it as he loathes his life. In a later scene the same thing happens. He runs up the stairs, and the post comes off. Only this time his reaction is the opposite. He covers that ugly hunk with kisses, grateful for both its beauty and its flaws.

The difference?

Gratitude.

It's a changed filter, a different perspective.

In the research literature this is actually called "The George Bailey Effect," based on a study that was reported in the *Journal of Social Psychology* in 2008 and cited by the *Wall Street Journal Health Journal*. In the study, college students were asked to write essays focusing on removing a particular positive event from their lives. They had to write as if it never happened. Another group of students simply wrote about a particular positive event. In the follow-up study, the researchers noted a modest "George Bailey Effect," in which the students who had to consider the subtraction of the positive event reporting being more grateful for the event than those in the other group.

As is the case with any good study, it supports biblical truth. Gratitude doesn't just fuel worship, as noted above in Colossians 3:16—it is also associated in wonderful combination with joy, gentleness, the lack of anxiety, peace, and hearts and minds that are guarded and safe. You'll find this powerful combination in Philippians 4:4-7.

> *Rejoice* in the Lord always. I will say it again: Rejoice! Let your *gentleness* be evident to all. The Lord is near. *Do not be anxious* about anything, but in everything, by prayer and petition, *with thanksgiving*, present your requests to God. And the *peace*

of God, which transcends all understanding, will *guard your hearts and your minds* in Christ Jesus (emphasis added).

In your Bible the subtitle for Psalm 100 may be something like "A Thanksgiving Psalm." And it starts, "Shout for joy to the Lord, all the earth" (Psalm 100:1). In 2 Corinthians 4:15 we see the imagery of a kind of thanksgiving that "overflows" because of God's grace. In Ephesians 5:4 the opposite of "obscenity, foolish talk or coarse joking" isn't love or rejoicing or encouragement; it's "thanksgiving."

There is a power in gratitude beyond the fact that it is polite, that it conforms to the norms of society.

We've already established the strong role your mind plays in chronic stress. The nature of gratitude is that it changes the way you perceive your world, the way you think. It forces your mind to turn from stressors and turn to blessings. "Finally, brothers and sisters, whatever is true, whatever is noble, whatever is right, whatever is pure, whatever is lovely, whatever is admirable—if anything is excellent or praiseworthy—think about such things" (Philippians 4:8) isn't just flowery poetic New Testament language. It's a rule for living, a key to stress reduction.

And it works. Journalist Melinda Beck studied research on the effect of gratitude and concluded,

> Being grateful also forces people to overcome what psychologists call the "negativity bias"—the innate tendency to dwell on problems, annoyances, and injustices rather than upbeat events. Focusing on blessings can help ward off depression and build resilience in times of stress, grief, or disasters, according to studies of people impacted by the September 11 terror attacks and Hurricane Katrina.[1]

Neal Krause conducted a study at the University of Michigan in which he concluded that older people who are grateful to God (specifically) have less stress.[2] Jo Musich, writing for the University of Minnesota, listed expressing gratitude as an important strategy for reducing stress related to the economy.[3] The American Heart Association recommends that you "practice gratitude" to reduce stress and blood pressure.[4] Beck continues—

> Adults who frequently feel grateful have more energy, more optimism, more social connections, and more happiness than those who do not, according to studies conducted over the past decade. They're also less likely to be depressed, envious, greedy, or alcoholics. They earn more money, sleep more soundly, exercise more regularly, and have greater resistance to viral infections.[5]

And it isn't only about being grateful, but practicing it as well. Feeling a sense of gratitude is important. It starts there; be thankful for God and His love, for the people around you, for the blessings in your life, for life itself. But an important exercise is *expressing* gratitude as often as possible. For your Father, that starts with praise, worship, and a life laid down—real surrender, in its greatest, most wondrous sense. Love someone? Say it. If you appreciate a person in your life, tell him or her, and specifically why you feel such appreciation. Appreciate a gesture? Mention it. And if you're the type who isn't always comfortable with a face-to-face interaction—although that's the ideal—there are multiple ways to communicate gratitude: notes, e-mails, texts, Facebook messages, tweets, blogs, flowers, candy. You get the idea. Perhaps if you've read or are reading a book that's helpful to you, send the authors a nice pie. We like pie.

Finally, one way to focus your gratitude and to train your mind against stress is to serve. Spend time helping others. It's likely that the best place to start is in your church family. If you haven't found a place to plug in and serve in your church, that's a ready-made opportunity. It helps if you can find service work in your church that others may not prefer, because that's often where the greatest good can be accomplished. "Each of you should use whatever gift you have received to serve others, as faithful stewards of God's grace in its various forms" (1 Peter 4:10). *The Message* paraphrase provides more details from the same text: "Be quick to give a meal to the hungry, a bed to the homeless—cheerfully. Be generous with the different things God gave you, passing them around so all get in on it."

It's no coincidence that after Peter's denial of his friend Jesus, and after the Lord's resurrection, Christ responded by putting Peter to work serving. Serving the people ("feed my sheep") is the way that Jesus first asked Peter to demonstrate his love. We suspect that a side benefit of Peter's work was helping him get back on track, his mind focused on serving. Further, in the sobering passage of Matthew 25, Jesus distinguishes the line between heaven and hell as what we have done "for the least of these."

Perhaps that's the greatest beauty of God's design for a heart that serves. It is His call on us and His will for us, but it also helps us. In his book *Thanks! How Practicing Gratitude Can Make You Happier*, Robert Emmons surveys the research that has been done on gratitude and the power of the practice of thankfulness. It is significant and impressive. God has designed us to be grateful and to express that gratitude. When we do, we're healthier. As he opens his work, Emmons quotes comedian and economist Ben Stein on the key to being rich: "I cannot tell you anything that, in a few minutes, will tell you how to be rich. But I can tell you how to feel rich, which is far better, let me tell you firsthand, than being rich. Be grateful. . . . It's the only totally reliable get-rich-quick scheme."[6] Emmons also concludes that being grateful and practicing gratitude are particularly powerful when we are going through the most difficult times in our lives. To be grateful when your life is full of trouble and pain has the power to change things, because it honors God by recognizing who He is. God works in and through you when you serve, particularly when you demonstrate faithfulness in your toughest times. Emmons points to the Pilgrims as examples of thanksgiving in times of trouble.

More than half of those courageous souls who crossed the Atlantic died after one year in their new home. . . . But they knew about ancient Israel's harvest festival: how Israel, at the end of a successful harvest, thanked God for the bounty of creation—and also for delivering them from their captivity, giving them their freedom as a people. And so they did the same. They understood their God to be a God who is to be thanked and praised when times are good and when times are tough. Their gratitude was not a selective, positive thinking facade, but rather a deep and steadfast trust that goodness ultimately dwells even in the face of uncertainty. Their thanksgiving was grounded in the actuality that true gratitude is a force that arises from the realities of the world, which all too often include heartbreak, sometimes overpowering heartbreak.[7]

There is a solid line connection between expressed gratitude, service, kindness, physical health, sleep, and mental well-being.[8] Those things tend to travel together, emphasizing again that isolation is a stressful and dangerous way to live.

. . . .

Consider

What are you grateful for in your life? Make a list. No, seriously, sit down and make a list, and be as detailed as you can possibly be. Start with things such as God's love for you, the opportunity for eternal life bought on the Cross, mercy. Then move to things such as family and friends. Be specific. "My daughter made me smile by drawing me a funny picture" is much better than "my daughter." "Martha accepts me for who I am" is better than "Martha." Don't forget to include little details like the sound of the ocean, the idea of chocolate, the ability to smile, the smell of fresh-baked bread, your favorite season, hot water, a pet that brings you joy, eating Chinese food with chopsticks, and so on. Be specific, and stretch yourself. Make the list as long as you possibly can. You should not stop until you're at least at fifty. Put it on your refrigerator, and set a goal that you will add at least one more item to your list every day for the next thirty days. You might want to write James 1:17 at the top of your list: "Every good and perfect gift is from above, coming down from the Father of the heavenly lights, who does not change like shifting shadows."

Ten

REST
THINK DIFFERENTLY TRUST GOD

*Blessed is the one who trusts in the LORD, whose confidence
is in him. They will be like a tree planted by the water that
sends out its roots by the stream. It does not fear when heat
comes; its leaves are always green. It has no worries
in a year of drought and never fails to bear fruit.*
—Jeremiah 17:7-8

● In 2007, the Hualapai Indian Tribe unveiled the Grand Canyon
Skywalk[1], a sightseeing bridge that juts out over the canyon. The
site is near Kingman, Arizona. If you go, you can walk out on the
horseshoe-shaped bridge and take in the gorgeous canyon views. The
Skywalk was built on the edge of the canyon and then rolled out into
place. It extends seventy feet over the edge, four thousand feet above
sea level and between five hundred and eight hundred feet above the
canyon floor. It is the largest cantilever glass bridge in the world.

You read that right—it's a *glass* bridge.

When you walk out on the bridge, you look down at your feet
and see nothing below them, with the exception of dirt and some
very hard rock a little less than a thousand feet away—down. The
Skywalk's builders make a point of trumpeting the soundness of
the structure. They tell you that the floor is four layers of Saint-

Gobain low-iron glass wrapped around what's called SentryGlas. It was made to withstand one hundred pounds per square foot as well as the heaviest of wind forces. They assure you that the structure is completely safe. Some even take a perverse joy in walking out on the bridge with the latest group of tourists and jumping up and down.

Pass.

We're talking about a glass bridge, eight hundred feet above the floor of the Grand Canyon! It is said that many arrive at the site with every intention of walking onto the bridge but think again and stay in the Skywalk's Welcome Center while other brave souls venture out.

Those who walk out on that bridge are putting their complete trust in its builders. They have faith that those builders knew what they were doing, that whatever state and federal inspections were done were thorough, that whatever testing was needed was completed. To walk out on that bridge, you must trust it. If it turns out to be worthy of your faith, you live. Otherwise—

Know it or not, like it or not, you trust God in the same way every day. Your life is at His whim (Colossians 1:16-17). He sustains you every minute of every day (Hebrews 1:3). Jesus doesn't just give life—He *is* Life (John 14:6). You may acknowledge that truth each day. You may think about it only occasionally. You may deny it. It's true—no matter.

The sparkle in this particular diamond is that God is trustworthy. You can trust Him, if you will. Our great worship pastor, Joseph, wrote a worship song that includes the line "Trusting you is easy, because you're so trustworthy."

For proof, look no further than Christ.

There was a point in time, about two thousand years ago, when your hopes were fading. True, you weren't around yet, but your destiny was hanging in the balance. People had proven that they couldn't live the life God designed, couldn't reach truth, faithfulness, or hope. They kept falling down, falling short. God had two choices at that time—either give up on us, dooming us to a forever-life without love, or do something about it. Make a way. Become *the* Way.

He chose the latter.

You know the story. He dispatched His Son as a rescuer. He was born on earth, lived life as a man—a perfect life—and grew up to die, to pay your ransom with His last breath. He was crucified, in effect building a bridge between you and God—the sturdiest of bridges, which you couldn't build on your own. He died, and that was it.

But it wasn't.

There was so much power in Him, so much love and hope that death couldn't hold on to Him past three days. He didn't stay dead but instead was resurrected, alive again. Many people saw Him living after dying, we suppose in case future doubters would come. His death and resurrection did what you couldn't do. Now He becomes the answer for anyone asking about love, hope, and life. He's your answer. And you can trust Him.

The Message presents Paul's version this way:

The first thing I did was place before you what was placed so emphatically before me: that the Messiah died for our sins, exactly as Scripture tells it; that he was buried; that he was raised from death on the third day, again exactly as Scripture says; that he presented himself alive to Peter, then to his closest followers, and later to more than five hundred of his followers all at the same time, most of them still around (although a few have since died); that he then spent time with James and the rest of those he commissioned to represent him; and that he finally presented himself alive to me (*1 Corinthians 15:3–8*).

Stress arises from the idea that none of this is true. Instead, you convince yourself—or someone does—that you cannot trust God. As a result, your life isn't in His hands because you won't put it there. Instead, it's all up to you. If that's what you believe, you likely will face chronic, debilitating stress. And that gets us back to your mind.

THINK DIFFERENTLY

We've addressed the relationship between the way you think and the level of your stress. We have referred to the Romans 12:2 text and the connection between your transformation and the "renewing of your mind." That old King James Version proverb "As he thinketh in his heart, so is he" (Proverbs 23:7, KJV) has turned out to be true. That is where "Think Differently" becomes an important part of the T in the REST model. Trusting God may call for the changing of your mind, thinking differently from the way you think now. The truth is, most people who think they're the solution to their own problems are actually the cause.

We suggest that there is a process to trusting God. First, start with the understanding that He is trustworthy. That is usually born out of regular consumption of His Word, teaching that is faithful to that Word, and interaction with people who trust Him. Practicing the REST model is also a way, not only to alleviate the negative effects of chronic stress but also to grow in trust.

Next, put trust into practice. The more you know God, the more you will trust Him. The opposite is true. You will not come to the point of trusting God unless you seek Him. You can't even find Him, as suggested by the well-known Jeremiah 29:11-14 passage:

"I know the plans I have for you," declares the LORD, "plans to prosper you and not to harm you, plans to give you hope and a future. Then you will call on me and come and pray to me, and I will listen to you. You will seek me and find me when you seek me with all your heart. I will be found by you," declares the LORD, "and will bring you back from captivity."

There are many great promises in the Bible. But "I will be found by you" has to be up there with the greatest. To find God, to know Him, is to trust Him.

How do you know if you're trusting God? Well, since it's a relationship, an expression of love, it's not an empirical science to be measured and codified, but there are signs. If you find yourself worrying less, you are likely trusting more. If your self-talk is more about your desperate reliance on God rather than your own potential for failure, there's faith happening there. If you're stepping out more, taking more risks in the interest of prayer, worship, discipleship, or evangelism, that's likely trust at work. Patience is another good sign. It usually grows with trust. As always, Oswald Chambers says it powerfully:

Patience is more than endurance. A saint's life is in the hands of God like a bow and arrow in the hands of an archer. God is aiming at something the saint cannot see, and He stretches and strains, and every now and again the saint says—'I cannot stand anymore.' God does not heed, He goes on stretching till His purpose is in sight, then He lets fly. Trust yourself in God's hands. Maintain your relationship to Jesus Christ by the patience of faith. "Though He slay me, yet will I trust in Him."[2]

Consider

Commit the following Scriptures to memory.

"Trust in the LORD with all your heart and lean not on your own understanding; in all your ways submit to him, and he will make your paths straight" (Proverbs 3:5-6).

"You will keep in perfect peace those whose minds are steadfast, because they trust in you. Trust in the LORD forever, for the LORD, the LORD himself, is the Rock eternal" (Isaiah 26:3-4).

"Without faith it is impossible to please God, because anyone who comes to him must believe that he exists and that he rewards those who earnestly seek him" (Hebrews 11:6).

It's probably best to memorize them one at a time, repeating and practicing until you can say them from your heart. Next, use them as weapons. Over the next week or so, whenever you begin to feel stressed, worried, or anxious about a particular occurrence, consider it to be an attack on your trust, and counterattack with one or all three of the Scriptures you've memorized. Tell your mind that you are choosing to trust and that your Rock is eternal and powerful, able to overcome anything you will face.

He is.

NOTES

Chapter 6

1. "America's No. 1 Health Problem," The American Institute of Stress, accessed April 14, 2012, <http://www.stress.org/americas.htm> (site now discontinued).

2. Seymour Levine, "Stress: An Historical Perspective," in *The Handbook of Stress and the Brain*, ed. T. Steckler, N. H. Kalin, and J. M. H. M. Reul (Amsterdam: Elsevier, 2005), 3.

3. Andrew Bernstein, *The Myth of Stress: Where Stress Really Comes From and How to Live a Happier, Healthier Life* (London: Piatkus, 2010), 4.

4. Ibid., 16.

5. Walter B. Cannon, *The Wisdom of the Body* (New York: W. W. Norton & Company, 1932).

6. Robert M. Sapolsky, *Why Zebras Don't Get Ulcers: An Updated Guide to Stress, Stress-Related Diseases, and Coping* (New York: W. H. Freeman and Company, 1998), 7.

7. Ibid.

8. Ibid., 22.

9. Mayo Clinic Staff, "Stress Management," Mayo Clinic, accessed April 17, 2012, <http://www.mayoclinic.com/health/stress/SR00001>.

10. Ibid.

11. Mary Carmichael, "Who Says Stress Is Bad for You?" *Newsweek,* February 13, 2009, <http://www.thedailybeast.com/newsweek/2009/02/13/who-says-stress-is-bad-for-you.html>.

12. Sapolsky, *Why Zebras Don't Get Ulcers,* 6.

13. Ibid.

14. M. Blake Hargrove, James Campbell Quick, Debra L. Nelson, and Jonathan D. Quick, "The Theory of Preventive Stress Management: A 33-year Review and Evaluation," *Stress and Health* 27, no. 3 (2011):186.

15. Sapolsky, *Why Zebras Don't Get Ulcers,* 13.

16. Mayo Clinic staff, "Stress Management."

17. Lisa Olen. "Mental Stress Advances Aging Process at Cell Level," *Daily News Central,* November 30, 2004, accessed April 17, 2012, <http://health.daily newscentral.com/content/view/000176/51/>.

18. Amber Keefer, "Top 10 Causes of Stress," livestrong.com, May 4, 2011, <http://www.livestrong.com/article/132015-top-10-causes-stress/>.

19. It's relevant to note that we don't read about fear in the first man until after we read about sin—Genesis 3:10.

Chapter 7

1. Sapolsky, *Why Zebras Don't Get Ulcers*, 7.

2. Bernstein, *The Myth of Stress*, 12.

3. Hargrove et al., "The Theory of Preventive Stress Management," 184.

4. The Romans 12:1-2 text reads, "I urge you, brothers and sisters, in view of God's mercy, to offer your bodies as a living sacrifice, holy and pleasing to God—this is your true and proper worship. Do not conform to the pattern of this world, but be transformed by the renewing of your mind. Then you will be able to test and approve what God's will is—his good, pleasing and perfect will." This section of Romans, taken as a whole, addresses more than just the power of the renewed mind, but it makes a powerful connection between a life of worship, a changed mind, and a life therefore lived in the good, pleasing, and perfect will of God.

5. Sapolsky, *Why Zebras Don't Get Ulcers*, 219.

6. Rebecca Coffey, "20 Things You Didn't Know About Stress," *Discover* 32, 5. 3 (2011), 2.

7. The story from Mark 4:35-41.

Chapter 8

1. Christine Gorman, "The Brain: 6 Lessons for Handling Stress," *Time*, January 19, 2007, <http://www.time.com/time/magazine/article/0,9171,1580401,00 .html>.

2. Sapolsky, *Why Zebras Don't Get Ulcers*, 216.

3. Ibid., 217.

4. Ibid., 143.

5. While the word is figuratively interpreted correctly as "deeply," "in earnest," or even "fervently," it is more literally "stretched out," which makes an interesting phrasing for how one person might love another and how that love is able to *cover* sin.

6. John 13:35.

7. Maria-Victoria Montes and Len Kravits, "Unraveling the Stress-Eating -Obesity Knot," *IDEA Fitness Journal* 8, no. 2 (2011):49.

8. Ibid.

9. Tara Parker Pope, "How Less TV Changes Your Day," *New York Times,* December 16, 2009, <http://well.blogs.nytimes.com/2009/12/16/how-less-tv -changes-your-day/>.

10. Ibid.

11. "Exercise for Stress and Anxiety," Anxiety and Depression Association of America, accessed April 14, 2012, <http://www.adaa.org/living-with-anxiety/ managing-anxiety/exercise-stress-and-anxiety>.

12. Some ideas from the Anxiety and Depression Association of America:

- 5 X 30: Jog, walk, bike, or dance three to five times a week for 30 minutes.
- Set small daily goals, and aim for daily consistency rather than perfect workouts. It's better to walk every day for fifteen to twenty minutes than to wait until the weekend for a three-hour fitness marathon. Lots of scientific data suggest that frequency is most important.
- Find forms of exercise that are fun or enjoyable. Extroverted people often like classes and group activities. People who are more introverted often prefer solo pursuits.
- Distract yourself with an iPod or other portable media player to download audiobooks, podcasts, or music. Many people find it's more fun to exercise while listening to something they enjoy.
- Recruit an "exercise buddy." It's often easier to stick to your exercise routine when you have to stay committed to a friend, partner, or colleague.
- Be patient when you start a new exercise program. Most sedentary people require about four to eight weeks to feel coordinated and sufficiently in shape so that exercise feels easier.

13. Larissa K. Barber and David Munz, "Consistent-sufficient Sleep Predicts Improvements in Self-Regulatory Performance and Psychological Strain," *Stress & Health: Journal of the International Society for the Investigation of Stress* 27, no. 4 (2011):314.

14. "Renew—Sleep and Stress," The Franklin Institute, accessed April 14, 2012, <www.fi.edu/learn/brain/sleep.html>.

15. Michael H. Bonnet and Donna L. Arand. "How Much Sleep Do Adults Need?" National Sleep Foundation, accessed April 17, 2012, <http://www.sleep foundation.org/article/white-papers/how-much-sleep-do-adults-need>.

16. The National Sleep Foundation website may be of help: <http://www .sleepfoundation.org/>.

17. John Tierney, "A Serving of Gratitude May Save the Day," *New York Times*, November 21, 2011, <http://www.nytimes.com/2011/11/22/science/a-serving-of-gratitude-brings-healthy-dividends.html>.

Chapter 9

1. Melinda Beck, "Thank You. No. Thank You," *The Wall Street Journal— Health Journal*, November 23, 2010, <http://online.wsj.com/article/SB100014240 52748704243904575630541486290052.html>.

2. Neil Krause, "Gratitude Toward God, Stress, and Health in Late Life," *Research on Aging*, February 17, 2006, <http://roa.sagepub.com/content/28/2/163 .full.pdf+html>.

3. Jo Musich, "Try Three Strategies to Reduce Stress over Economy," University of Minnesota Extension, February 23, 2009, accessed April 2, 2012, <http://www.extension.umn.edu/extensionnews/2009/strategies-reduce-stress.html> (site now discontinued).

4. "Step 5: Prevention and Treatment," American Heart Association, accessed June 2, 2012, <http://www.heart.org/HEARTORG/Conditions/High BloodPressure/PreventionTreatmentofHighBloodPressure/Stress-and-Blood -Pressure_UCM_301883_Article.jsp>.

5. Beck, "Thank You. No. Thank You."

6. Ben Stein, *I Cannot Tell You Anything*, American Gratitude, The American Enterprise, 18-21, quoted in Robert Emmons, *Thanks! How Practicing Gratitude Can Make You Happier.* (New York: Houghton Mifflin, 2007), 1.

7. Emmons, *Thanks! How Practicing Gratitude Can Make You Happier,* 186.

8. John Tierney, "A Serving of Gratitude May Save the Day," *New York Times*, November 21, 2011, <http://www.nytimes.com/2011/11/22/science/a-serving-of -gratitude-brings-healthy-dividends.html>.

Chapter 10

1. You can see a video of it at <http://www.youtube.com/watch?v=KJrv6pkci0 I&feature=related> or <http://www.youtube.com/watch?v=BvzlZuWrJNw>.

2. Oswald Chambers, "The Faith to Persevere," *My Utmost for His Highest*, accessed May 7, 2012, <http://utmost.org/the-faith-to-persevere/>.